CW00644546

Best wishes Howard

Phil Bateman

May 2002.

CREWE WORKS
in the Age of Steam

A Pictorial Tribute
by Edward Talbot

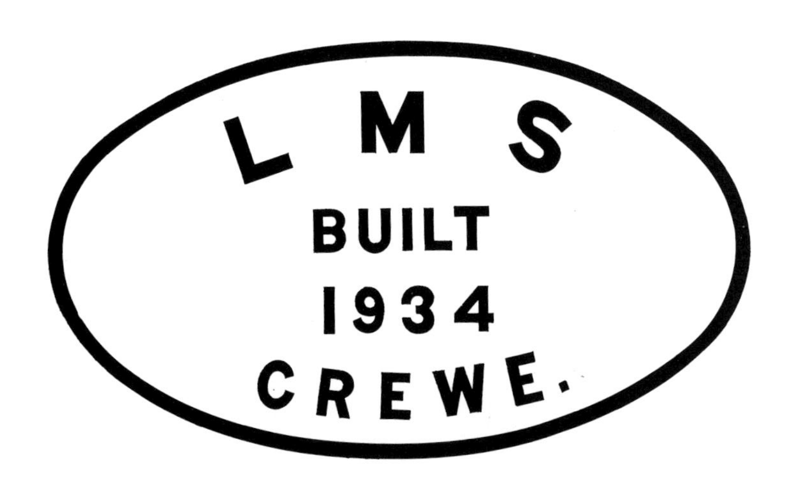

Edward Talbot

Oxford Publishing Company

Title page: LMS Crewe Works plate. *Courtesy Alan Gettings*

Frontispiece: A general view looking west towards the Steel Works from the top of the water tank in Flag Lane, sometime in the 1890s. In the left foreground is the stone yard bank, centre left is the main Chester line, running between two walls isolating it completely from the works, and beyond the Chester line, reached by the Eagle Bridge, is the Carriage Works. The left-hand set of six chimneys serves the melting furnaces, generally referred to as 'The Melts'. They were supplied with raw materials by means of the tracks leading up the ramp to them. Special cut-down versions of Mr Webb's '2ft. 6in. Shunters' worked on this line, serving the 20 ton furnaces night and day from 1890 until at least the 1920s. One of them can be seen in the lower left foreground, waiting while a gang of men loads 'pigs' (bars of pig iron) on to a wagon, no doubt, to be fed into the furnaces. Beyond 'The Melts' is the rail mill, which supplied all the LNWR's requirements for rails. The buildings in the centre right house the foundry and the forge, in which area can be seen a set of sheer legs. Out of the picture, on the right, is the paint shop.

Raw materials of all kinds are stacked all over the site ready for use — coal, pigs, bricks, timber, stone and pipes, and no doubt several others which are now difficult to identify. Many of these materials would be used for manufacturing, but others are for the maintenance of the Works itself. Most of the work of unloading these materials from wagons delivering them to the Works, stacking them in their storage areas, loading them again to be transported to wherever they were required, and unloading them on site, was done by hand, by gangs of labourers employed for the purpose. The only mechanical aids, apart from one or two fixed cranes, were Mr Webb's 0-4-2 'Crane Tanks', two of which can be seen at work, loading supplies on to wagons. All in all, a fascinating glimpse of late Victorian industry.

Foreword to this Impression

Prior to the passing of the Railways Act 1993, which provided the foundation for the full privatisation of the railways, British Rail Engineering was one of the first major railway businesses to be transferred to the private sector in 1989, as BREL Limited. The new owners were the Swiss/Swedish electrical engineering group ABB (Asea Brown Boveri), civil engineers Trafalgar House, the management team and it's employees.

Change continued to take place and as a result of the movement from Classified Exams to Cost Effective Maintenance, fewer locomotives were shopped for repair. However there was a considerable increase in the number of major assemblies sent in for overhaul from other works and depots around the country. In 1990 the last locomotives to be built in Crewe, the Class 91s, were completed and released to revenue earning duties.

ABB Transportation took overall control in 1992 and the workshops continued to develop as a Centre of Excellence for component overhaul, providing increasingly reliable equipment for the soon-to-be-privatised fleets.

With the turn of a New Year, 1996 brought a further change of ownership and automotive giant Daimler-Benz acquired a 50% stake in the company; the name Adtranz being derived from the two groups owning the business. ABB handed complete control to the newly created DaimlerChrysler Rail Systems company two years later. Despite fears due to constant change, the worldwide headquarters for Customer Support activities was established in Crewe in 1998. The workshop activities and management philosophies were held up as the standard to which all other operations, across the globe, would aspire.

A visit to the factory today would give the observer an image of a business ever changing to meet the needs of the modern railway and contemporary business philosophies. A new entrance has been created at the east end, close to the old Goddard Street gate. The old foundry has been replaced by a supermarket and petrol station. Gone are the myriads of small buildings and gantries. Locomotives are no longer built and much of the fabrication and machining is subcontracted. The image presented is much cleaner, sharper and focussed.

Ownership is now with Bombardier, a French-Canadian Corporation whose rail transportation business is viewed as a core activity. Each night over 100 tonnes of components are despatched from the Crewe Central Logistics Warehouse to depots and factories across the United Kingdom, to support the rail network. In addition there is the ever continuous overhaul of wheels, bogies, traction-motors, generators and power units for the High Speed Trains and also naval vessels.

The tradition of Open Days has continued to be extremely popular, so much so that the 2000 event was held over a full week-end. Over 20,000 people attended to view the 55 steam, diesel and electric locomotives on display. Poignantly, one of the exhibits was *Pet*, an original narrow gauge loco which hauled loads within the Crewe complex from 1845 to 1929.

The operation in Crewe will continue to change to meet the needs of train operators at home and abroad well into the 21st century and that it does so is a testament to the solid foundation of engineering expertise which has been provided and developed by the many craftsmen, engineers and staff who worked at 'the Works' over the previous 158 years.

Phil Bateman,
Crewe
May 2001

Introduction

Early in the nineteenth century, the facts of geography had already determined that Crewe would be a major junction on the future railway system. It was the obvious place for lines to Manchester and Chester to join the main line between Birmingham and the north. Before the railway was built, the site of that junction was merely an uninhabited part of rural Cheshire. Soon, however, the spot was destined to be much more than a mere junction. The far sightedness of the Directors of the Grand Junction Railway, and in particular of their brilliant young Engineer, Joseph Locke, led to the construction of the company's locomotive works there. In time it was to grow into one of the greatest industrial complexes the world has ever seen.

Nowadays, very little of the original Works remains. The 'Old Works' has been demolished entirely and much of the site has been redeveloped. The General Offices, no longer needed, were abandoned and were soon destroyed by fire; what survived of the building has also since been demolished. The Deviation Works too has been demolished. These buildings would have been ideal for conversion to a railway museum. Indeed, if their potential had been fully appreciated locally, the National Railway Museum, now at York, could have had no better location, but the opportunity has now been lost, along with all the benefits which tourism would have brought to the town of Crewe and the surrounding area. The newer part of the Works, of course, still survives. Modernised and transformed to meet the needs of diesel and electric locomotives, it is now a sizeable asset of British Rail Engineering Limited.

The 150th anniversary of the opening of the Grand Junction Railway occurs on 4th July 1987, and provides a fitting opportunity to recall the great days of the railway at Crewe. This book is therefore intended as a contribution to the celebrations. It is designed as a pictorial tribute to Crewe Works in the age of steam, and above all to the many generations of men at all levels, whose skill, energy and vision made that great enterprise possible.

Edward Talbot
Stafford
1986

Bibliography

There are three excellent books on Crewe Works:

Chaloner, W. H, *The Social and Economic History of Crewe*, Manchester University Press 1950, reprinted 1973.

Reed, Brian, *Crewe Locomotive Works and Its Men*, David & Charles, Newton Abbot, 1982.

Reorganisation of Crewe Locomotive Works, The Railway Engineer, 1929

First published 1987
Reprinted 1987 and 1988
This impression 2001

ISBN 0 86093 395 4

Published by Oxford Publishing Co

an imprint of Ian Allan Publishing Ltd, Hersham, Surrey KT12 4RG.
Printed by Ian Allan Printing Ltd, Hersham, Surrey KT12 4RG.

Code: 0106/2

Historical Survey

During the age of steam, Crewe Works was the leading railway works in the country, and for a time, in the whole world. As well as building and repairing locomotives and carriages, it manufactured dozens of other items needed by the railway, items as diverse as steel rails and needles, bricks and gas mantles, signals and lubricants; it even produced soap from the grease in the dirty cloths returned by the steam sheds for washing. Moreover, it trained hundreds of men in locomotive and railway engineering. Some of them, on qualifying, worked for the company itself, some went to other British companies and very many went to railways overseas, in the British Empire and beyond. Thus Crewe practice spread all over the globe. In 1913 *The Railway Magazine* rightly described Crewe Works as 'the most famous railway works in the world'.

Crewe Works was first built by the Grand Junction Railway, the first main-line railway in the country, in the 1840s. The Grand Junction had been mooted as long ago as the 1820s, but it was not until 6th May 1833 that the Grand Junction Railway Act finally received the Royal Assent. This Act authorised the 'making of a railway from the Warrington & Newton Railway at Warrington in the County of Lancaster to Birmingham in the County of Warwick.' The Grand Junction Railway derived its title from the fact that it connected Birmingham with the Liverpool & Manchester Railway at Newton Junction. Its title became even more appropriate when the London & Birmingham Railway was completed, as it then linked the four largest cities in the country.

Initially, George Stephenson was appointed Engineer in charge of the construction of the line, with Joseph Locke and John Urpeth Rastrick as his immediate assistants. Owing to personality differences, however, Stephenson took less and less interest in the work and eventually resigned. Shortly beforehand, in August 1835, Joseph Locke was appointed Chief Engineer. He was barely 30 years of age.

The Grand Junction Railway was exceptional among early railways, and indeed among major engineering projects of any era, in that it was completed on time, for which much of the credit belongs to Locke. The official opening took place on 4th July 1837, when the engine *Wildfire* hauled the inaugural train from Birmingham to Liverpool. There were first-class stations at Birmingham, Wolverhampton, Stafford, Crewe, Hartford and Warrington. First-class trains stopped only at these stations but 'mixed' trains, catering for both first and second-class passengers, also stopped at the intermediate stations.

The original works of the GJR was built alongside that of the Liverpool & Manchester Railway at Edge Hill. Its location, away from the company's own metals, is an indication of the close co-operation between the two railways from the outset. The site was too restricted, however, for further development, and in June 1840 the Directors resolved to build a new works 'at the junction of Crewe' for 'the building and repairs of carriages and waggons as well as engines'. The site was chosen because it offered ample space at the focal point of the company's system. Crewe was not only a convenient place on the main line, but from early days was clearly destined to be a major junction. Lines to Chester (and so to Holyhead and Ireland), to Manchester (and so to Leeds and the West Riding), to Shrewsbury (and so to Central and South Wales) and to Stoke on Trent (and so to the East Midlands) were soon projected, and built.

The original works was built in open country on a triangular site formed by the main line to the north and the line to Chester. Streets of houses were built close by, to accommodate the men who worked there and their families, and other amenities were also provided by the company, including Christ Church. Thus, there came into being the town of Crewe. The completion of the Works was celebrated by a great ball and banquet on 2nd December 1843. In later years, to distinguish it from subsequent developments on other sites, this Works came to be known as the 'Old Works'. In 1845, the Grand Junction Railway amalgamated with the Liverpool & Manchester Railway, and in 1846 it amalgamated with the London & Birmingham Railway to form the London & North Western Railway. These, and subsequent changes over the years, led to more and more work being concentrated at Crewe.

The first expansion out of the original site occurred almost immediately. By 1854 an iron-rail mill, tender shop, and joiners and pattern-makers shop had been built opposite the Old Works on the south side of the Chester line. During 1848/9 new shops for carriage repair and painting were built on the other side of the main line to the north. They were parallel with the main line, and were linked to the Old Works by a footbridge across the tracks. Further east, on the same site, flanking the Manchester line, was built a smithy, a timber yard and a plant for the manufacture of grease for lubricating axleboxes. The shops on this site soon came to be referred to as the 'Grease Works'. These developments were the natural consequences of the policy of self-sufficiency which the company practised from the very beginning. Facilities were installed, usually at Crewe, to manufacture any item which could be produced more cheaply than it could be bought from an outside supplier.

At first the works was responsible for carriage building and repairs, but in 1859 new construction was transferred to Saltley. The carriage shops at the Old Works then changed to locomotive work, but the carriage shops on the Grease Works site continued to carry out repairs.

As traffic grew and the company's system developed, Crewe Works was enlarged to cope with the increasing demands on its facilities. In the 1860s expansion took place on two new sites. Firstly, the far-sighted decision was taken that the company should have its own Bessemer steel-making plant. The site chosen was north of the Chester line, east of Flag Lane, and the new plant was in production in 1864. This site had plenty of room for expansion, and over the years many other shops were added. Some took over functions previously performed at the Old Works but others, such as the brick kiln, were new enterprises. In official literature, the term 'Steel Works' often encompasses not just the steel-making plant itself but also all the various other shops and facilities on the same site. In a sense, this part might have been called the 'New Works', to distinguish it from the original or Old Works, but that term has never been used. In modern times it is this site that anyone referring to 'Crewe Works' generally has in mind.

The second new site that was developed in the 1860s was the result of the increasing inconvenience which was caused by having shops on both sides of the Chester line. This line had to serve the Works as well as carry busy traffic in its own right. It was therefore decided to bypass the Works entirely, by building a new Chester line on the south side. The original line then served the Works only; the new line, opened in 1868 and known as the 'deviation', had no connection to the Works at all. More shops were then built at the eastern end of the land bounded by the old and new lines, and came to be known as the 'Deviation Works'. When these shops were completed in the late 1860s, a general reorganisation took place, and some of the functions previously performed by the Old Works were transferred to the Deviation Works.

By this time the original offices under the clock tower in the Old Works had become quite inadequate, and so new offices were built parallel to the old Chester line east of Chester Bridge. They were opened in 1876 and were known as the 'General Offices', being invariably referred to in the town as the 'G.O.'. Their situation was conveniently central to the various sites of the Works, but also gave easy access to the town.

The next and final development on a new site was the construction of a new Carriage Works south of the main Chester line east of Flag Lane — in effect, on the opposite side of the line from the Steel Works. When this new works was completed in 1878, the carriage shops at the Grease Works were closed. They were demolished in the late 1890s to make way for the 'up' goods avoiding line, built as part of the reconstruction of Crewe Station, which was completed in 1906. The new Carriage Works was responsible only for repairs; the construction of new carriages was now concentrated at Wolverton. Access to the Carriage Works was not direct from the Chester line but from the Steel Works by means of the Eagle Bridge. This bridge was so called because on each of the four corners of its abutments were mounted large cast-iron eagles, which had arrived as scrap for the Steel Works and had been considered worth saving.

Near the Carriage Works was the ash tip, where slag from the Steel Works was dumped, and on the same site, but a little further west, were the cooling ponds for the rail mill in the Steel Works on the north side of the line. To the south-west was the Gas Works, which supplied both the Works itself and the town. This works was opened in the 1870s and replaced the original Gas Works on the south side of the original Chester line at the Old Works.

Henceforward new developments were largely concentrated on the Steel Works site. A new paint shop was completed in the north-east corner of the site in 1878, and in subsequent years various other shops were built, modernised and reorganised, from time to time. For instance, the original Bessemer plant was replaced by more modern steel-making facilities, and along the north side of the Steel Works site was built a third line of shops in the late 1870s and early 1880s. From east to west these were the steel foundry, iron forge, spring mill, axle forge and erecting shops Nos. 5-8. Later, the west end of all the shops on the site was extended, No. 8 erecting shop on the north side, the boiler shop on the south side and the plate store in between. In 1903 a new erecting shop, No. 9, and a fitting shop were built west of the central group of shops in the Steel Works complex. North of these shops was the open-air storage area for boilers, on the east side of which was the road leading from the main Works entrance in West Street.

During World War I, much of the productive capacity of the Works was turned over to the manufacture of munitions. Because resources were concentrated on the war effort, normal renewal and maintenance of plant and machinery was neglected, and similarly the standard of maintenance of essential railway equipment, such as locomotives, declined. When the war ended, it was clear that major reorganisation and modernisation of the Works was required. Nothing was done immediately, however, partly because of the organisational problems resulting from the amalgamations of the early 1920s. On 1st January 1922, the London & North Western Railway merged with the Lancashire & Yorkshire Railway, and a year later the combined company became part of the London Midland & Scottish Railway.

The much-needed reorganisation took place in the mid-1920s. A major part of the scheme was the construction of a large new erecting shop on the south side of No. 9 erecting shop. Officially, this shop was No. 10 erecting shop, but it was also known as 'erecting shop south'. The various other erecting shops were then altered to other functions, and reference to the 'erecting shop' then signified only this shop.

The new shop was a great improvement on previous erecting shops. It was much better equipped, with better cranes, and was much more spacious. At first, an attempt was made to apply production line methods to engine repair work, in a system which was known as 'the belts'. Previously, each engine had been the responsibility of one gang of men. They dismantled it on arrival, performed all the operations required to repair it, went on its trial trip, and made any adjustments as a result of it. Now each gang performed only certain operations. An engine for repair entered the shop and was added to one of the lines of engines which were already being worked on. At fixed time-intervals the whole line of engines was moved forward from one gang to the next by means of a winch at the end of the shop. As each engine passed out of the shop, its overhaul was complete. The system was not entirely successful, largely because different classes differed in the time needed for the various operations. Eventually it was abandoned, in the form in which it was originally conceived, but the new erecting shop continued to be a considerable asset to the Works.

After this reorganisation, Crewe Works reached its maximum development. Certain facilities, such as the manufacture of steel, were closed down in the 1930s, as the LMS abandoned the old LNWR principle of self-sufficiency in favour of buying from outside suppliers. Nevertheless, the Works remained essentially in this form throughout World War II, when again much war work was done, up to the nationalisation of the LMS on 1st January 1948, and throughout the early British Railways period until the final demise of steam in the 1960s.

Plate 1: Opposite the General Offices was this old milepost, erected at the time when the line through the Works was the original Chester line. It must have been put up before the Trent Valley line was opened in 1846, as it shows the mileage to London as 167, the distance by the Grand Junction Railway, via Birmingham. The post survived at least into the 1960s. Behind it is the 'coppice', a man-made hillock covered in bushes and trees, and intended to shield the view of the Deviation Works from the gardens of the homes of the LNWR officers in Chester Place, and from the General Offices.

A Crewe Works Chronology

1833 6th May; the Grand Junction Railway Act received the Royal Assent. George Stephenson appointed Engineer in charge of construction.
1835 August; Joseph Locke appointed Engineer in place of George Stephenson.
1837 4th July; inauguration of the Grand Junction Railway. First-class stations at Birmingham, Wolverhampton, Stafford, Crewe, Hartford and Warrington. Locomotive Works at Edge Hill, Liverpool.
1840 June, William Barber Buddicom appointed Locomotive Superintendent; Alexander Allan appointed 'foreman of the workshops'. The Directors resolve to build a new Works 'at the junction of Crewe'.
1841 Construction of 2-2-2 engine No. 26 *Aeolus* at Edge Hill. The double-frame outside-cylinder design was developed by Locke and Buddicom, and was the forerunner of what later came to be known as the 'Old Crewe' type.
August; Buddicom resigned as Locomotive Superintendent — replaced by Francis Trevithick.
1843 October; first engine to be built at Crewe completed, No. 32 *Tamerlane.* 2nd December; completion of Crewe Works celebrated with a ball and banquet.
1845 July; No 49 *Columbine,* the first 'standard' 6ft. 2-2-2, completed — traditionally regarded as the first engine to be built at Crewe Works and now preserved as No. 1868 at the National Railway Museum, York.
Grand Junction Railway amalgamated with the Liverpool & Manchester Railway.
1846 Grand Junction Railway amalgamated with the London & Birmingham Railway to form the London & North Western Railway.
18571st August; John Ramsbottom appointed Locomotive Superintendent of the LNWR Northern Division at Crewe.
1858 September; the 'DX' class 0-6-0 introduced. By the early 1870s 943 had been built, the most numerous British locomotive class.
1859 November; the 'Problem' or 'Lady of the Lake' class 2-2-2 introduced.
1862 1st April; Ramsbottom appointed Locomotive Superintendent of the whole LNWR. McConnell, formerly Superintendent of the Southern Division at Wolverton, resigned.
May; *Tiny* completed, the first engine for the Crewe Works internal 18in. gauge railway.
1866 December; completion of 'DX' class 0-6-0 No. 613, officially the 1,000th engine built at Crewe.
1871 September; John Ramsbottom resigned due to ill health; replaced by Francis William Webb from 1st October.
1874 December; the 'Precedent' class 2-4-0s introduced.
1876 August; the 2,000th engine built at Crewe, Webb 2-4-0 tank No. 2233.
1878 August; Trevithick 2-2-2 No. 54 *Medusa* converted to work as a two-cylinder compound, No. 1874, Webb's first experiment in compounding.
1887 June; the 3,000th engine built at Crewe, 2-2-2-2 compound tank engine No. 600. 'Improved Precedent' or 'Large Jumbo' class introduced.
1889 March; 'Teutonic' 2-2-2-0 class introduced, the most famous and successful Webb compounds.
1892 October; the first eight-coupled goods engine completed, No. 2524.
1893 September; the first three-cylinder compound 0-8-0 completed, No. 50.
1900 March; the 4,000th engine built at Crewe, 'Jubilee' class four-cylinder compound 4-4-0 No. 1926 *La France.*
1903 May; F. W. Webb retired and replaced by George Whale as Chief Mechanical Engineer from 1st July.
1904 March; 'Precursor' class 4-4-0s introduced.
1909 George Whale retired and replaced by C. J. Bowen Cooke from 1st July.
1910 July; the first superheated engine completed, 'George the Fifth' class 4-4-0 No. 2663 *George the Fifth.*
1911 June; the 5,000th engine built at Crewe, 'George the Fifth' class 4-4-0 No. 5,000 *Coronation.*
1912 February; 'G1' class 0-8-0 superheated goods engine introduced, the famous 'Super D'.
1913 January; 'Claughton' class express passenger 4-6-0s introduced.
1914-19 Crewe Works heavily involved in the production of munitions for World War I.
1920 18th October; C. J. Bowen Cooke died; replaced as Chief Mechanical Engineer by H. P. M. Beames from 1st November.
1922 1st January; LNWR merged with Lancashire & Yorkshire Railway. George Hughes of the LYR appointed Chief Mechanical Engineer of the combined system.
1923 1st January; formation of the London Midland & Scottish Railway. Beames remained as Mechanical Engineer, Crewe, until retirement in 1934.
1926 Crewe Works reorganised, No. 10 erecting shop built, 'the belts' system of repairs introduced.
1930 June; 'Horwich Crab' 2-6-0 No. 13178, renumbered 2878 in 1934, officially declared the '6,000th' engine built at Crewe (although in fact Fowler 7F 0-8-0 No. 9517, built in May 1929, had Crewe motion number 6000).
1933 June; No. 6200 *The Princess Royal* completed, the first Stanier Pacific.
1935 February; the first 'Class 5s' built at Crewe (although preceded by the Vulcan Foundry batch built in 1934).
1937 June; streamlined 'Princess Coronation' class introduced for working 'The Coronation Scot' high-speed train — first engine No. 6220 *Coronation.*
1943 June; 'Rebuilt Royal Scot' class introduced — first engine No. 6103 *Royal Scots Fusilier.*
1950 September; the 7,000th engine built at Crewe, Ivatt Class 2, 2-6-2 tank No. 41272.
1951 January; the first BR standard engine completed, 4-6-2 No. 70000 *Britannia.*
1954 January; the first BR 9F 2-10-0 completed, No. 92000.
1958 December; the last steam engine built at Crewe, BR 9F 2-10-0 No. 92250. It was officially calculated to be the 7,331st engine built at Crewe, but historians have estimated it to be more like the 7,357th.
1967 2nd February; the last steam engine to be repaired at Crewe, 'Britannia' class 4-6-2 No. 70013 *Oliver Cromwell,* left the Works.

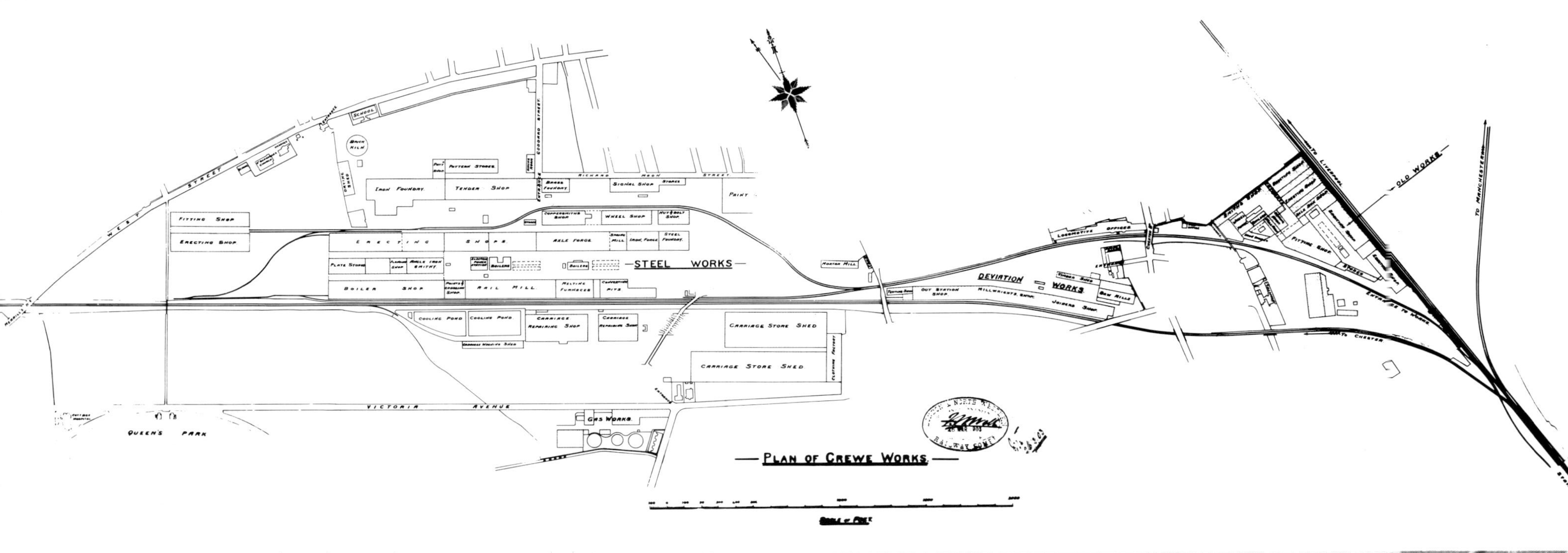

Figure 1: The official plan of Crewe Works dated 26th March 1903 and signed by F. W. Webb himself. The Grease Works, between the main line to the north and the Manchester line, has been omitted, and the new erecting shop, built at the extreme west end of the Steel Works site in the 1920s, is also, of course, not shown. With these two exceptions, the map shows the Works at its maximum development.

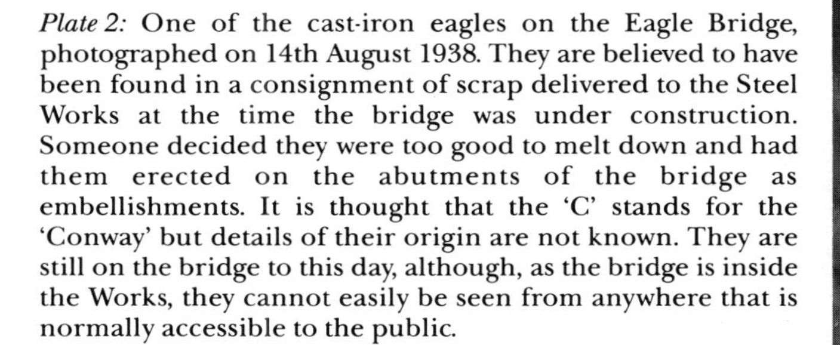

Plate 2: One of the cast-iron eagles on the Eagle Bridge, photographed on 14th August 1938. They are believed to have been found in a consignment of scrap delivered to the Steel Works at the time the bridge was under construction. Someone decided they were too good to melt down and had them erected on the abutments of the bridge as embellishments. It is thought that the 'C' stands for the 'Conway' but details of their origin are not known. They are still on the bridge to this day, although, as the bridge is inside the Works, they cannot easily be seen from anywhere that is normally accessible to the public.

Plate 3: A general view of the Old Works, looking north, probably circa 1880, with the main line to the north on the right. It seems that the photograph was taken on some special occasion, in view of the flags that are flying, but exactly what is not known (possibly the visit of the Shah of Persia in 1873). Early photographs of locomotives were taken in front of the buildings on the left. Most of them had the clock tower as a prominent feature — in this picture it is obscured to some extent by flags. The buildings on the right originally served as a running shed ('steam shed' in LNWR parlance), as can be seen from their roofs, but they are now erecting shops. On the extreme right is the footbridge leading to the Grease Works.

Plate 4: The clock tower of the Old Works, in a somewhat decrepit state, in the 1960s.

Plate 5: A view from Crewe North Junction signal cabin looking north-east up the Manchester line in 1881, and showing the Grease Works. On the extreme left are the carriage shops built during 1848/9 and demolished in the late 1890s as part of the reconstruction of Crewe Station. To the right of them are the timber yard, smithy and Grease Works proper.

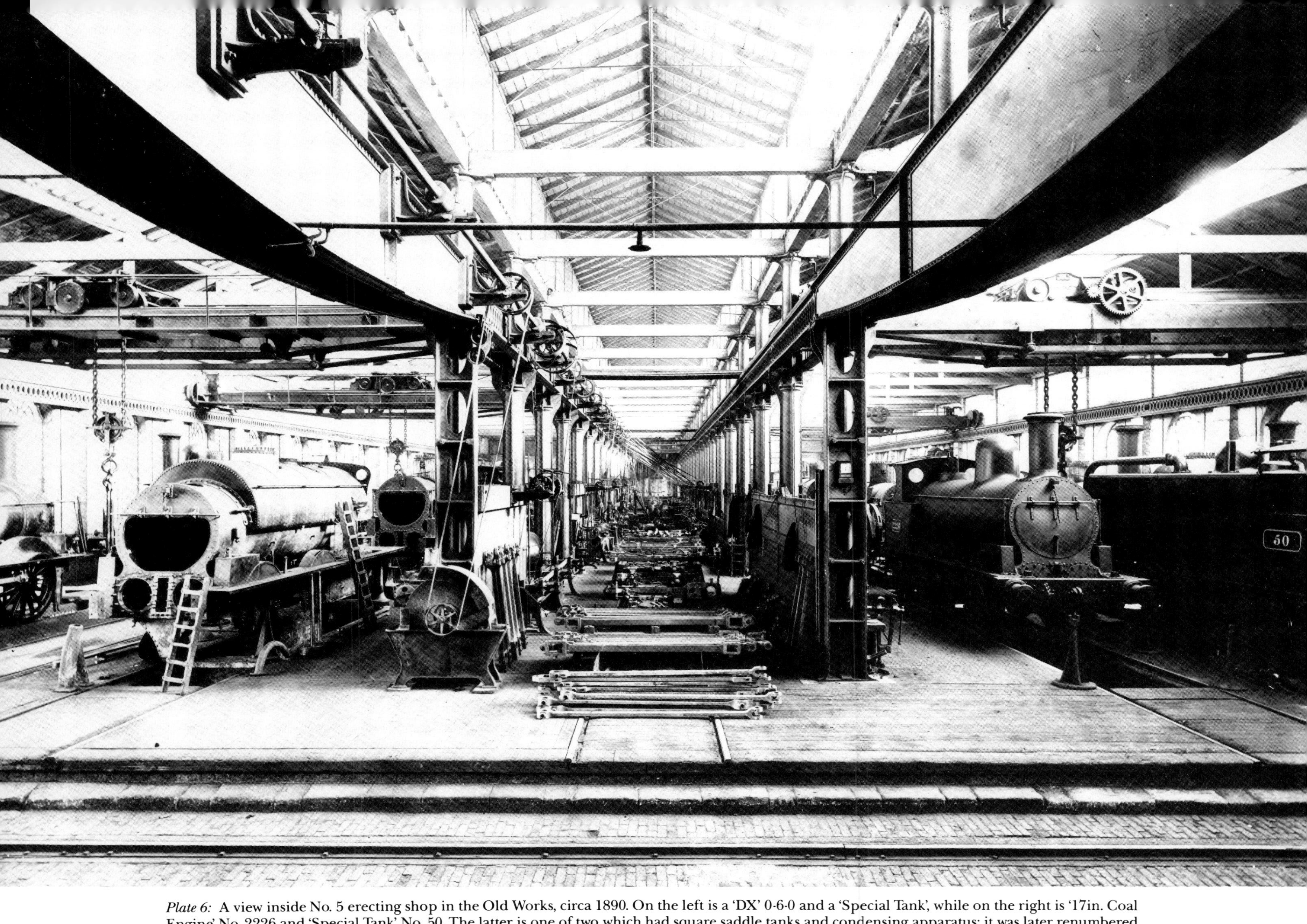

Plate 6: A view inside No. 5 erecting shop in the Old Works, circa 1890. On the left is a 'DX' 0-6-0 and a 'Special Tank', while on the right is '17in. Coal Engine' No. 2226 and 'Special Tank' No. 50. The latter is one of two which had square saddle tanks and condensing apparatus; it was later renumbered 3021 and named *Liverpool*. In the centre is the arcade containing machines and work benches, and used, at this end at least, for preparing rods for fitting. In the foreground is the track of the traverser.

Plate 7: A view inside No. 4 erecting shop in the Old Works in the early 1900s. A wooden gantry crane has collapsed, apparently through overloading. Its 'crab' (the machine holding the hook and moving back and forth on the gantry) has fallen on the bunker of an engine, an '18in. Tank', whose rear end it appears to have been lifting. The other end is still attached to the other crane. The cranes are driven by ropes running along pulley wheels mounted on the wall, and powered by a steam engine at the end of the shop. At first glance, the picture is somewhat confusing, with the broken crane and the engines so close together (an impression that is increased by the foreshortening effect of the camera) but it repays careful study. As well as interesting detail of the cranes and the shop, it shows engine parts that are not often seen, such as the steam collection pipe in the dome and the V-shaped steam chest.

The four pictures which follow are interior views of the Old Works. Those of the machine shops were taken on 30th March 1906, and that of the fitting shop on 9th December 1899. Although at first glance puzzling, with a maze of machines and belts packed closely together, they are again worth close study for the insight they give into Victorian engineering practice. Working conditions are now hard to imagine but the din of the overhead shafting, the drive belts and machines must have been deafening. Equally impressive is the quality of the photography, inside such poorly and unevenly lit shops; results of this calibre would not be easily achieved today.

Plate 8: The machine shop, with a group of small lathes used for making brass fittings.

Plate 9: The north-east corner of the machine shop. On the right is a vertical borer being used for milling, and near the centre is a slitting saw. Two groups of castings, probably for hydraulic equipment (the shops did not just make parts for locomotives) are well in evidence.

Plate 10: The fittting shop, where parts made in the machine shop were brought to be assembled. Among various items that can be distinguished, are more hydraulic pumps on the left, coupling and connecting rods, and reversing wheels in the middle distance.

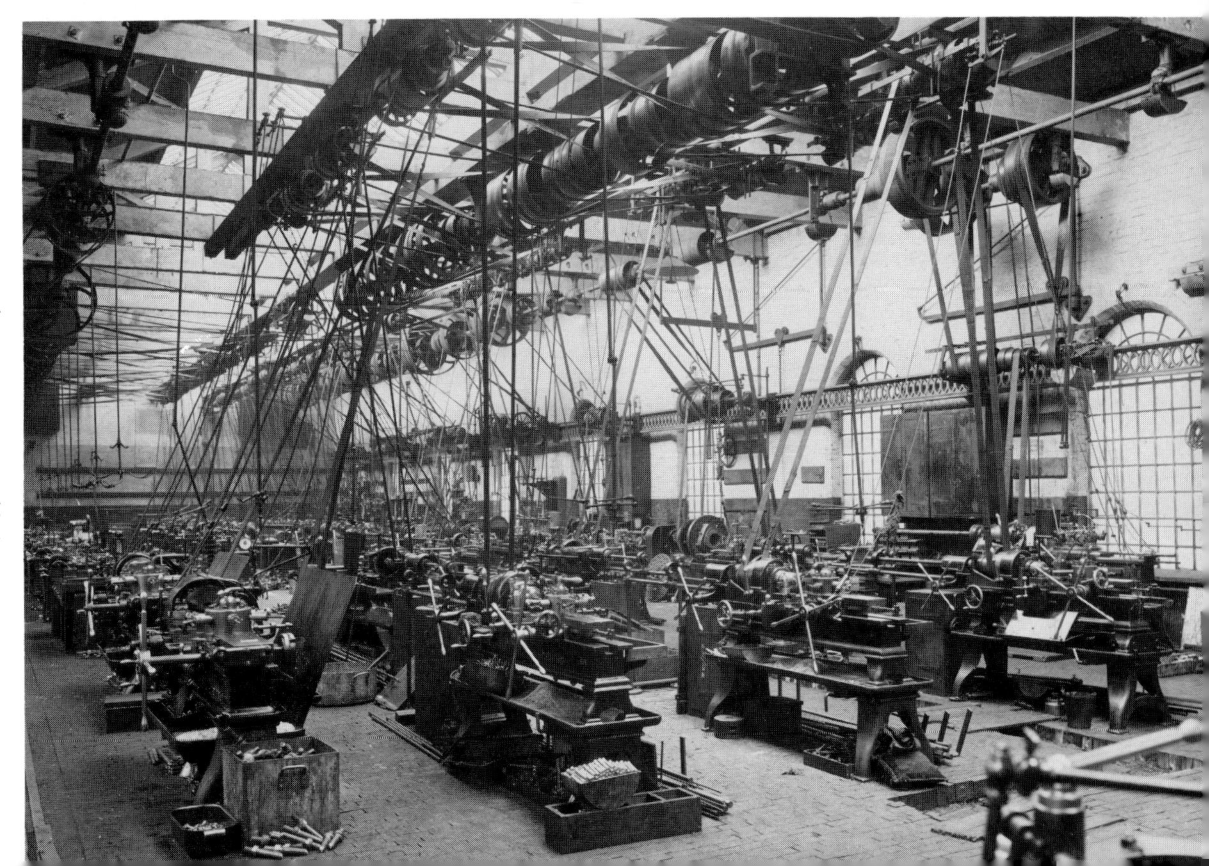

Plate 11: A group of turret lathes in the machine shop. This view shows clearly, on the left, the gas lights above the machines, fed by pipes running along the roof beams; they are the open-flame type of light. On the right can be seen the ropes enabling the operator to start and stop the belt drive to his machine; probably there is some sort of dog clutch on the overhead shafting.

An Engine Built in 25½ Hours

To show what the Works could achieve, in February 1878, '17in. Coal Engine' No. 2153 (described officially as a '4ft. 3in. Coal Engine', from the size of the driving wheels) was erected in only 25½ hours. Some accounts say that it was not only erected in that time but was also in steam. These five photographs show the various stages in the engine's construction.

Plate 12: The main frame plates laid out for the photographer before erection began. The fittings on the wall are open-flame gas lights.

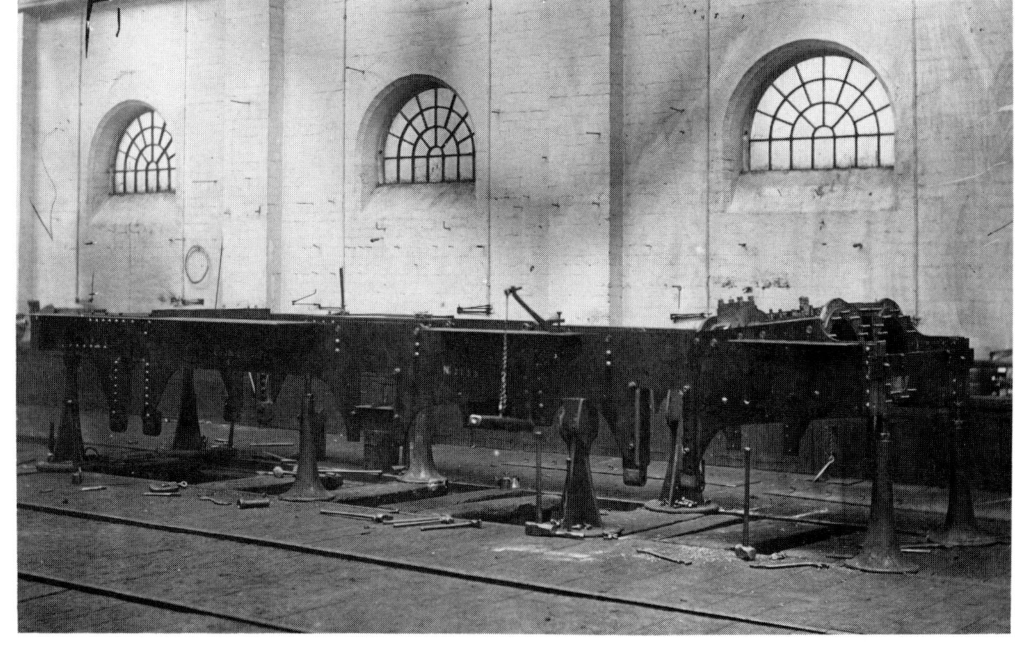

Plate 13: The frames erected on stands, the stretchers riveted up, and the cylinders secured in the frames with fitted bolts. The rear hornblocks have already been riveted into the frames, while the leading ones are held in position with bolts before being riveted.

Plate 14: The boiler, steam turret and cab side-sheet, with the ashpan in position under the firebox ready to be attached; part of the motion is installed between the frames and the ash chute is fitted beneath the cylinders. A hand-powered ratchet drill is being used on the centre horns.

Plate 15: The completed engine, wheeled and with all fittings installed.

Plate 16: The engine posed with the men who constructed it. On the right is the gang of platers; they are holding riveters' tongs, caulking hammers and a riveter's dolly. On the left are the fitters, with hammers and files. In front of both gangs are ratchet drills. On the extreme left is F. W. Webb himself, in the cab is George Dingley, the erecting shop foreman, and fourth from the left is C. J. Bowen Cooke, then an apprentice in the Works. In the background is the recently completed building of the General Offices — the ivy has yet to grow up the walls. A more commonly published version of this photograph has this background painted out. In later years, many engines were photographed further to the left, with the trees in the officers' gardens as background, but this is the only official photograph taken at this location. Perhaps the 'coppice' had not then been made, or perhaps the photographer decided that painting out this background regularly was too difficult.

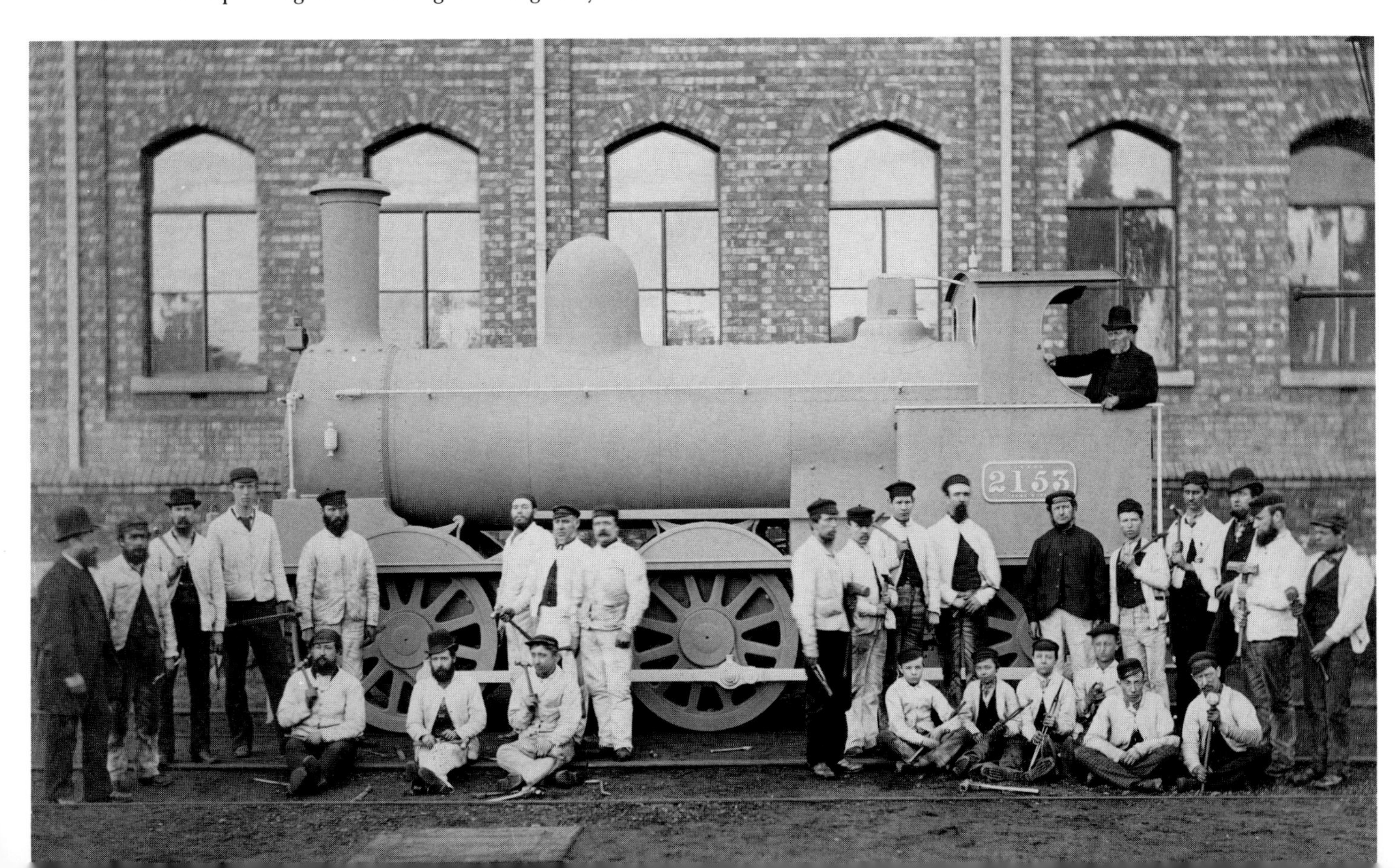

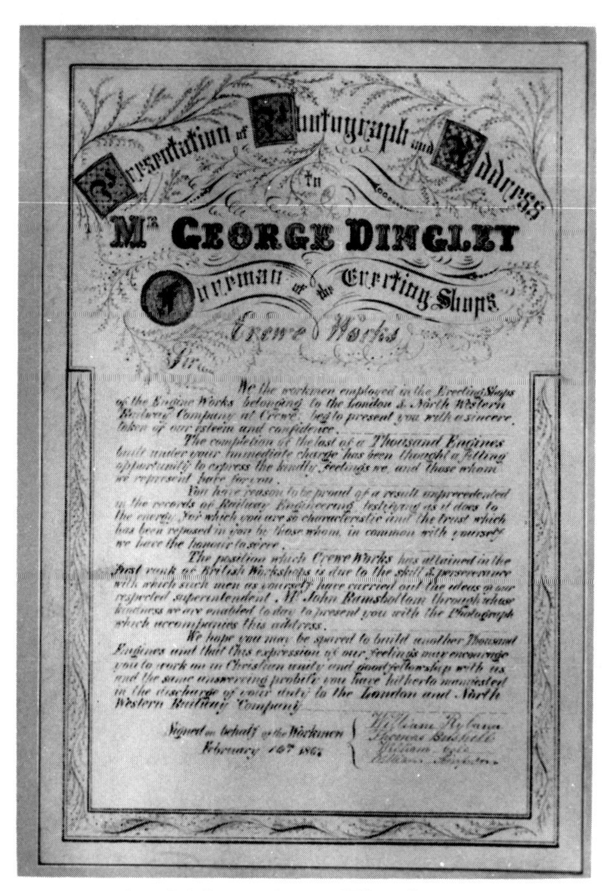

Presentation of Photograph and Address to Mr George Dingley Foreman of the Erecting Shops Crewe Works

Sir

We the workmen employed in the Erecting Shops of the Engine Works belonging to the London & North Western Railway Company at Crewe beg to present you with a sincere token of our esteem and confidence.

The completion of the last of a Thousand Engines built under your immediate charge has been thought a fitting opportunity to express the kindly feelings we and those whom we represent have for you.

You have reason to be proud of a result unprecedented in the records of Railway Engineering testifying as it does to the energy for which you are so characteristic and the trust which has been reposed in you by those whom, in common with yourself we have the honour to serve.

The position which Crewe Works has attained in the first rank of British Workshops is due to the skill & perseverance with which such men as yourself have carried out the ideas of our respected superintendent, Mr John Ramsbottom through whose kindness we are enabled to day to present you with the Photograph which accompanies this address.

We hope you may be spared to build another Thousand Engines and that this expression of our feelings may encourage you to work on in Christian unity and good fellowship with us and the same unswerving probity you have hitherto manifested in the discharge of your duty to the London and North Western Railway Company.

Signed on behalf of the Workmen February 16th 1867

Plate 17: When the 1,000th engine to be built at Crewe Works was completed, 'DX' class 0-6-0 No. 613, the men employed at the Works presented the erecting shop foreman, George Dingley, with an illuminated address. It is reproduced here, along with a transcription of the text.

Presentation of Photograph and Address
to
Mr George Dingley
Foreman of the Erecting Shops
Crewe Works

Sir

We the workmen employed in the Erecting Shops of the Engine Works belonging to the London & North Western Railway Company at Crewe beg to present you with a sincere token of our esteem and confidence.

The completion of the last of a thousand engines built under your immediate charge has been thought a fitting opportunity to express the kindly feelings we and those whom we represent have for you.

You have reason to be proud of a result unprecedented in the records of Railway Engineering, testifying as it does to the energy for which you are so characteristic and the trust which has been reposed in you by those whom, in common with yourself, we have the honour to serve.

The position which Crewe Works has attained in the first rank of British Workshops is due to the skill & perseverance with which such men as yourself have carried out the ideas of our respected superintendent, Mr John Ramsbottom, through whose kindness we are enabled today to present you with the Photograph which accompanies this address.

We hope you may be spared to build another Thousand Engines and that this expression of our feelings may encourage you to work on in Christian unity and good fellowship with us, and the same unswerving probity you have hitherto manifested in the discharge of your duty to the London and North Western Railway Company.

Signed on behalf of the workmen
February 16th 1867

William Rylance
Thomas Bushell
William Cole
William Simpson

From the Old Works to Flag Lane

AS the LNWR system expanded and traffic increased, so Crewe Works needed to be enlarged to cope with the growing demands made upon it. Room for expansion was simply not available at the Old Works, and in the 1860s the Steel Works was built on a site west of Flag Lane and north of the Chester line. At about the same time, the decision was taken to build a new line to Chester, bypassing the Works entirely. Some new shops were built parallel to the new line at the west end of the area bounded by the new and old lines, and so came to be known as the Deviation Works. The pictures which follow show the route along the original Chester line between the Old Works and Flag Lane bridge, at the east end of the Steel Works site. Several of them were taken during the Royal Visit in April 1913, and can easily be distinguished by the various decorations put up in honour of the visit.

Plate 18: A view looking through the 'iron bridge' towards the Old Works, on the left, and Crewe Station. The building on the left, beyond the bridge, houses the smiths' shop and the wheel forge. In the sidings are engines awaiting shopping. They will be brought up to the Steel Works area by one of the Works' shunters, as required. On the far left is the footpath leading to the Forge Street entrance. In the centre is the weigh-house, with a 'Jumbo' standing just beyond it. The gas lamps now have mantles.

Plate 19: A view looking in much the same direction as the previous picture but from a much higher viewpoint, the top of the Plaza Cinema in High Street, and much later, circa 1960. The shed of the weigh-house is on the left, and the buildings of the Old Works take up most of the picture. Two LMS standard '3F' 0-6-0 tanks are on Works shunter duties.

Plate 20: The entrance to the Old Works at the corner of High Street and Mill Street, on 12th September 1963, with '3F' 0-6-0 tank No. 47597 on duty. To the right was the Works hospital.

Plate 22 (left): The pay office, circa 1960, with LMS standard '3F' 0-6-0 tank No. 47646 shunting in the foreground. The pay for the whole Works was made up in this office and was then distributed.

Plate 21 (left): A view looking the other way, through the 'iron bridge' towards Chester Bridge and the General Offices. The righthand arch of the bridge houses the 'Coupé and Steam Fire Engine'. The coupé was the Chief Mechanical Engineer's saloon, which had its own small platform under the arch. Stairs led directly to this platform from just inside the main entrance to the General Offices by Chester Bridge. Above the centre arch of the bridge is the legend 'Loyal Welcome'. Hidden by the weigh-house on the right of the picture is the pay office.

Plate 23 (right): The main entrance to the General Offices by Chester Bridge, decorated for the Royal Visit. The model of *Rocket* in the window is now in the entrance to Crewe Station.

Plate 24: The General Offices, seen from a coal train passing under Chester Bridge towards the Steel Works.

Plate 25 (above left): Groups of visitors to the Works were common. They often posed for their photograph by the steps of the main entrance to the General Offices from the old Chester line. This group is from India, His Highness the Ihahore Saheb of Morbi being seated at the front. Standing at the rear is F. W. Webb, in a sense royalty himself, being styled by some the 'King of Crewe', and not without good reason.

Plate 26 (below left): Another group, the Prime Minister of Uganda, Apolo Kagma, and his party, standing by the Chief Mechanical Engineer's coupé by the entrance to the offices on 26th July 1902. F. W. Webb is leaning on the buffer of the coupé. The lamps have been changed from the previous picture but the fine boot-scrapers remain.

Plate 27: The General Offices, looking towards Chester Bridge (out of the picture on the right), on 26th July 1898.

Plate 28: Next to the General Offices were the company houses, occupied by LNWR officers employed at Crewe. Here, in 1885, by the entrance to No. 1 Chester Place, the residence of the Chief Mechanical Engineer, is a group which includes John Ramsbottom, the former Locomotive Superintendent, third from the right, and F. W. Webb, the Chief Mechanical Engineer himself. The title of the post changed during the latter's period in office.

Plate 29: Another group in the garden of Chester Place, this time members of the Iron and Steel Institute, on 29th September 1910. In the centre of the group, behind each other, are Sir Gilbert Claughton and C. J. Bowen Cooke.

Plate 30: A group of 'past and present Crewe pupils and premiums' in the garden of Chester Place, on 27th May 1927. Of the four gentlemen on the front row, the second from the left is H. P. M. Beames, the last Chief Mechanical Engineer of the LNWR, and the fourth, H. N. Gresley, later Sir Nigel Gresley, the Chief Mechanical Engineer of the LNER. Crewe Works trained large numbers of apprentices over the years but only a very small proportion of them obtained posts with the company on completing their training. Some went to other British and Irish companies but many went overseas to railways in India, Africa and South America, and to various parts of the British Empire.

Plate 31: Crewe Works military band in the garden of one of the official residences in Chester Place, on 8th August 1921. Their uniforms have Britannia on the cap badge and engines on the collar.

Plate 32: The gardens of the official residences came up to the old Chester line, and the trees and shrubs in them created a background which was popular with the official photographers over many years for taking pictures of locomotives. In this view '2ft. 6in. Shunter' No. 3017, an 0-4-0 well tank fitted for oil-burning, is posed broadside in the traditional location, on 27th July 1896. A gardener is standing on the path leading from the houses to a gate in the wall, giving the officers direct access from their homes to the Works. Above the engine is the tower of St. Mary's Catholic Church — the house is Windycotes.

Plate 33: Here, LMS No. 13088, a 'Horwich Crab' but built at Crewe, is posed a little further west, with the lines leading into the Deviation Works in the foreground, on 3rd October 1927. The engine would still perhaps have seemed somewhat strange at Crewe, in its LMS maroon livery, but nevertheless must have been a magnificent sight.

Plate 34: This view of LMS No. 6100 *Royal Scot*, splendidly prepared for its tour of the USA in 1933, is a little unusual in that it shows the line leading past the General Offices and the 'coppice' on the right. The engine is not in fact the original *Royal Scot,* but No. 6152, which was in more suitable condition for the tour. Similarly its tender, although of the same general outline as the Fowler tenders normally coupled to the 'Scots', is actually the third Stanier tender to be built, No. 9002. It holds 4,000 gallons of water and 9 tons of coal, by comparison with the 3,500 gallons and 5½ tons of the Fowler tenders. The first two Stanier tenders were fitted to the first two 'Princess Royals', Nos. 6200 and 6201, and the fourth to the 'Turbomotive' No. 6202.

Plate 35: Another fine sight, 'Rebuilt Claughton' 4-6-0 No. 5927 *Sir Francis Dent* in the traditional location on 9th October 1928. It is fitted with Caprotti valve gear.

Plate 36: After World War II, the LMS decided not to revert to maroon, and BR adopted green for express passenger engines and LNWR lined black for mixed traffic. To the delight of many, however, twenty Stanier Pacifics were painted maroon in the late 1950s, and this picture of 'Coronation' class No. 46254 *City of Stoke-on-Trent* shows the wisdom of the decision. The engine has been specially prepared for an exhibition at Stoke-on-Trent Station in 1960, in celebration of the fiftieth anniversary of the elevation of the 'Five Towns' to the status of 'city'.

Plate 37: For the same occasion the paint shop also turned its hand to North Staffordshire Railway livery in restoring an Adams Class 'L' 0-6-2 tank, which had been in industrial service at Walkden Colliery, Lancashire.

Plate 38: A view approaching Flag Lane bridge from the General Offices. The points in the left foreground are the junction for the lines leading to the Deviation Works. Through the bridge, the main line to Chester is behind the wall; the tracks going straight on lead to the south side of the Steel Works and those to the right lead round to all the shops on the north side of the Steel Works and to the paint shop.

Plate 39: A view looking in the opposite direction through Flag Lane bridge. The path on the left leads to the General Offices; the train is standing on the junction with the line to the Deviation Works, which is on the right. The shop immediately on the right is the chain shop.

Plate 40: Photographs of the Deviation Works seem to be so rare as to be virtually non-existent. This view shows the interior of the 'electric light station' at the Deviation Works, on 9th May 1903. The electric generator sets (modern parlance) seem to be powered by twin-cylinder compound reciprocating steam engines; they were built at Crewe but are closely similar to engines made by outside firms such as Belliss & Morcom of Birmingham. Webb was a pioneer in the use of electricity, both for lighting and to drive machines in the Works. In a speech in 1896, he foresaw the electrification of the Euston to Carlisle main line, and spoke of speeds of 100m.p.h.

The Carriage Works

Plate 41: A scene in the Carriage Works Yard on 17th March 1912, on the occasion of the last parade of the Volunteer Railway Engineer Corps, often referred to as the 'Crewe Volunteers', which were disbanded by order of the War Office when the Territorial Army was created. On the left is the band, and on the right, in civilian clothes, the veterans. Assorted LNWR and West Coast Joint Stock carriages, parcel vans and fish vans are in the centre of the picture. Behind them are the walls on both sides of the Chester line, and beyond them can be seen the tops of various shunting engines employed in the Works. The Eagle Bridge, with its nameboard, is directly beneath the chimney just off centre to the left. The 'Crewe Volunteers' or 'Crewe Engineers', as they were also known later, paraded in the Market Square, where other photographs were taken. Photographs of the Carriage Works are extremely scarce, interior views being virtually non-existent.

Plate 42: A view of the Steel Works, photographed from the tower of the Catholic Church in Delamere Street, on 5th July 1895 during the Works' holiday. It shows roughly the same scene as the *Frontispiece* but includes more on the right, in particular the distinctive north-light roof of the paint shop, with its sixteen roads. Above it, to the right, is the Bessemer Hotel.

Plate 43: Although technically a poor picture, it is one of some interest, being taken in the yards east of the Steel Works. Much of the foreground is occupied by piles of 'pigs' (bars of pig iron), while on the right are circular blocks of something, with loops in the top to enable them to be lifted by the 'Crane Shunter' behind. Beyond the engine is the Eagle Bridge, and to its left is the Carriage Works.

Plate 44: Work proceeding on the construction of the rail mill in 1874. The chimneys on the right belong to the original Bessemer steel plant of the early 1860s. On the left is the original boiler house, which has had a water tank added on top of it.

Plate 45: One of the Bessemer converters, on 23rd January 1894. It was tilted to a roughly horizontal position to be charged with materials and then turned back to the vertical before the blast was applied, its 'exhaust' passing up the flue to the right. Another converter can be seen in the right background. The man centre right has one hand on the control lever of the crane which would hold the ladle from which molten steel would be poured into the moulds seen in the picture, to make ingots. On the right are both narrow and standard gauge tracks. The narrow gauge wagon is carrying two ingots, which are no doubt about to be taken, while still hot, for rolling, probably in the rail mill. Four other wagons are stacked by the crane.

Plate 46: The rail mill on 4th July 1895, after being altered to produce 60ft. rails. On the right is the cogger, while on the left, are the triple-decker rollers. Electric lighting is already installed. The first steel rails were made at Crewe probably in 1862.

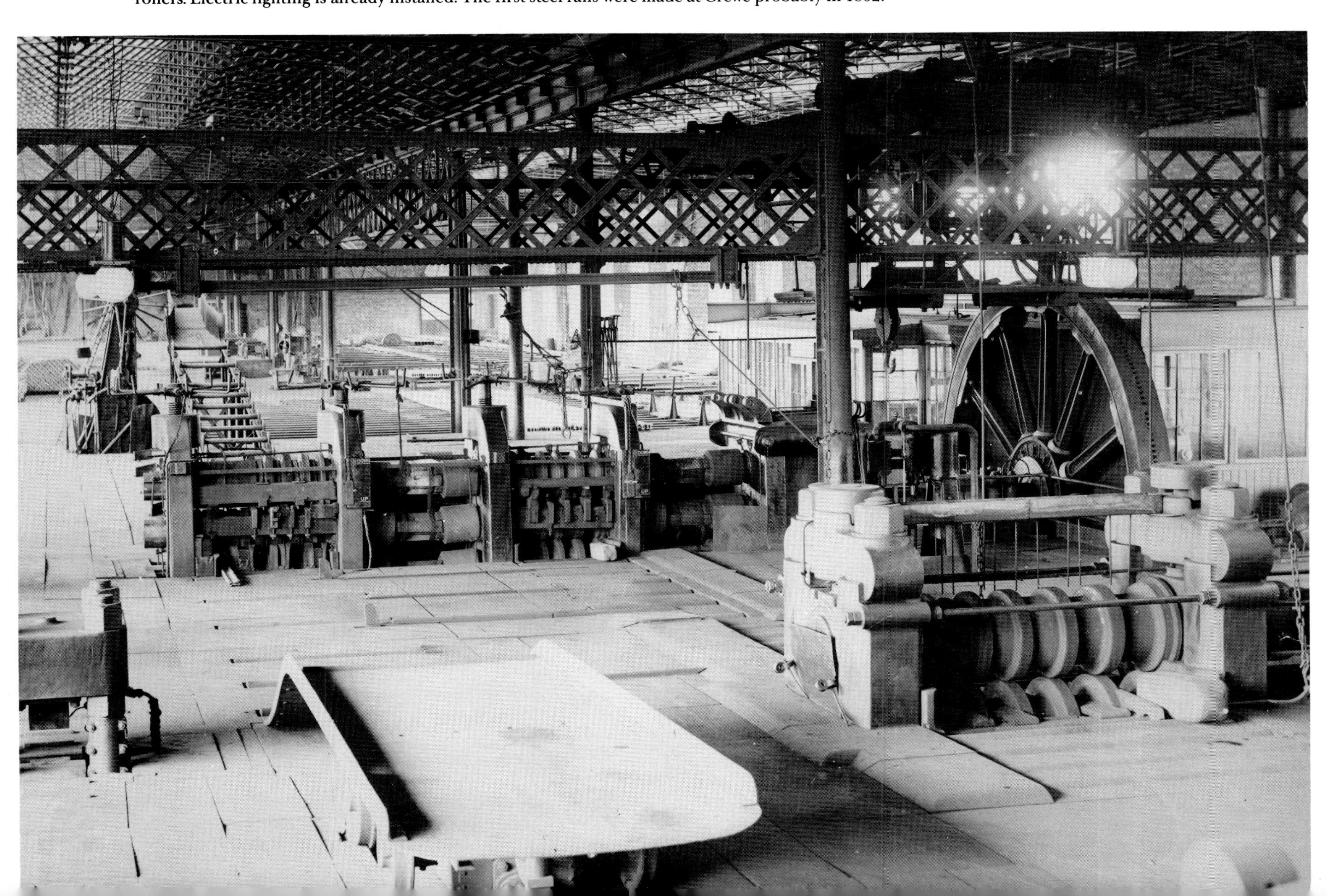

Plate 47: The iron foundry on 30th December 1899. In the centre are two jib or pivot cranes, across the same bay is a crane operated by hand from the floor by means of chains, and high up on the left are two rope-operated cranes. Their drivers could only reach them by means of the ladders visible in the picture, which were then removed by men on the ground. Moulds, patterns and core-boxes are well in evidence, while hanging up on the right are two sieves, used for the moulding sand. The track running the length of the building was to carry the ladle of molten metal from the furnace and to take out the finished castings. In the wall, centre right, is the drying oven for making cores. On the widened part of the crane gantry runway is the plaque commemorating the opening of the foundry. It is still in the same position today.

Plate 48: Two men peering into one of the furnaces just before tapping, on 12th March 1931. Steel production at Crewe ceased shortly afterwards.

Plate 49: Permanent way, steel sleepers laid with rails, all made entirely at Crewe, in August 1879. The rear rail bears the legend 'L&NWR CREWE STEEL'. In the background is the wall of the paint shop, not long completed.

Plate 50: An improved version of the steel sleeper, with flattened ends, and photographed in May 1886.

Plate 51: A view of part of the forge in 1896. The boiler and cylinders of an old engine provide power for the machinery. In the foreground are the tracks of the narrow gauge system.

Plate 52: A hydraulic forging press in the Steel Works, in 1897.

Plates 54, 55, & 56 show views inside the fitting and machine shops at the Steel Works.

Plate 55: (above): Axleboxes being produced on the same date.

Plate 56 (below): Perhaps also on the same date, rods being machined. Prominent in the foreground is a connecting rod for Joy's valve gear.

Plate 53 (above left): The engine providing hydraulic power for the forging press, in 1897.

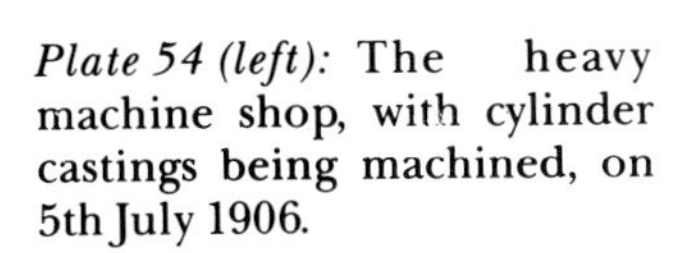

Plate 54 (left): The heavy machine shop, with cylinder castings being machined, on 5th July 1906.

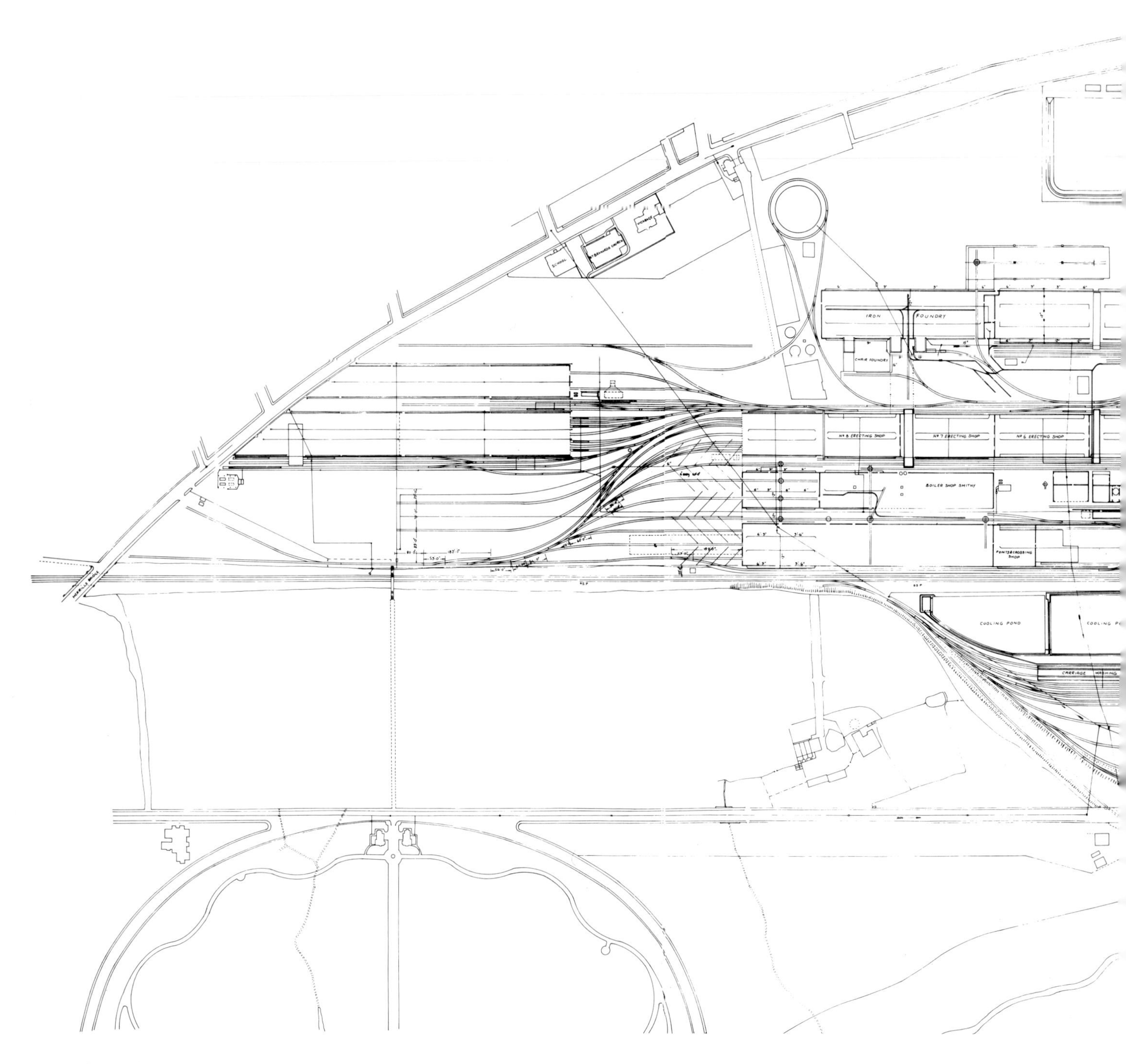

Figure 2: Plan of the Steel Works site about 1910. A particularly noteworthy feature is the extensive nature of the narrow-gauge system. It was to last in this form until the reorganisation of the mid-1920s.

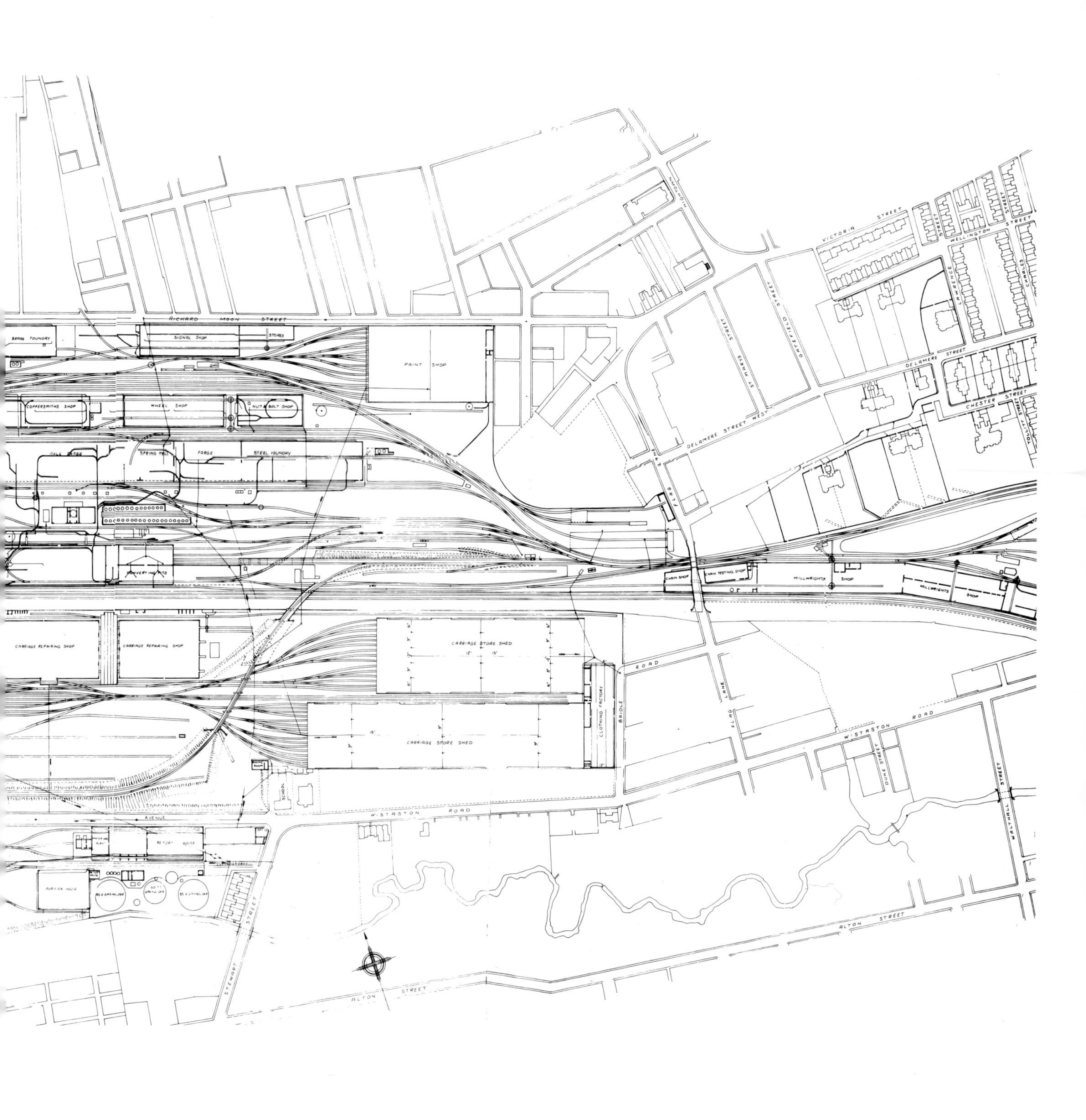

RICHARD MOON STREET
BRASS FOUNDRY
SIGNAL SHOP
STORES
PAINT SHOP
COPPERSMITHS SHOP
WHEEL SHOP
NUT & BOLT SHOP
SPRING MILL
FORGE
STEEL FOUNDRY
CONVERTING PITS
CARRIAGE REPAIRING SHOP
CARRIAGE REPAIRING SHOP
CARRIAGE STORE SHED
CARRIAGE STORE SHED
CLOTHING FACTORY
BRIDLE ROAD
FLAG LANE
CHAIN SHOP
CHAIN TESTING SHOP
MILLWRIGHTS SHOP
MILLWRIGHTS SHOP
DELAMERE STREET WEST
ST MARYS STREET
VICTORIA STREET
WELLINGTON STREET
LAWRENCE STREET
DELAMERE STREET
CHESTER STREET
W.STASTON ROAD
DUKE STREET
WALTHALL STREET
ALTON STREET
STEWART STREET
AVENUE
RETORT HOUSE
PURIFIER HOUSE
SCHOOL

The Boiler Shop

Plate 57 (left): The boiler shop on 4th January 1900, probably photographed from the crane at the end of its run. In the centre are boilers for the smaller Webb classes, while on the left are larger boilers, used probably on eight-coupled coal engines. Some way down the shop can be seen the riveting tower, with a boiler vertically in position for riveting.

Plate 58 (below left): Another view of the boiler shop on the same occasion, but looking from the riveting tower towards the end of the shop.

Four views of the boiler shop, photographed on 14th September 1934.

Plate 59 (right): A boiler at the riveting tower. The boiler is stood on end, resting on a turntable, which moves it into the required position for riveting. Three holes were drilled simultaneously.

Plate 60 (below): A firebox wrapper being formed by a machine which bent it to the required shape in one operation.

Plate 61: Riveters at work on a firebox, using a pneumatic riveting machine. The noise was literally deafening.

Plate 62: Two men at work screwing in stays through the firebox wrapper.

Machines

Plate 63: The period after John Ramsbottom became Locomotive Superintendent, in 1857, was one of rapid and considerable development. Not only did he expand and reorganise the shops, but he also revolutionised the manufacture of locomotives by introducing better methods and processes and by inventing new machines. This machine, brought out of the shop on the traverser for photography, is a typical example. Driven by ropes, its purpose was to grind the surfaces of the hornblocks. It is seen here set up to dress all twelve faces on the frames of a 'DX' class 0-6-0 simultaneously, in July 1877.

Plate 64: A hydraulic press for carriage wheels, in 1883.

Plate 65: A wheel lathe, in 1892.

Erecting Shops

Plate 66: In the late nineteenth century, new erecting shops, numbered 5-8, were built on the north side of the complex of shops at the Steel Works. This is the view inside No. 8 shop at about the turn of the century, showing two Webb four-cylinder compound 'Jubilee' class 4-4-0s under repair. The one on the right is No. 1901 *Jubilee* itself. Its driving wheels are in the centre of the picture — the pockets to hold balance weights on the inner side of the boss can be seen. The crane is electric; the down-shop leads can be seen on the wall. The gas lights on the left-hand wall are the open-flame type, and are supplied by pipes running down the wall.

Plate 67: Another view inside No. 8 erecting shop, with 'Jubilee' class four-cylinder compound 4-4-0s under construction. On the left is No. 1908 *Royal George*, which seems to have already been in service and has probably been brought into the shop as an example of the finished version of the engines being built. Interesting detail of its cab can be seen, and the frames on the right are also of interest, in showing detail of their construction, the main frames being secured to the cylinder castings by vertical lines of large bolts.

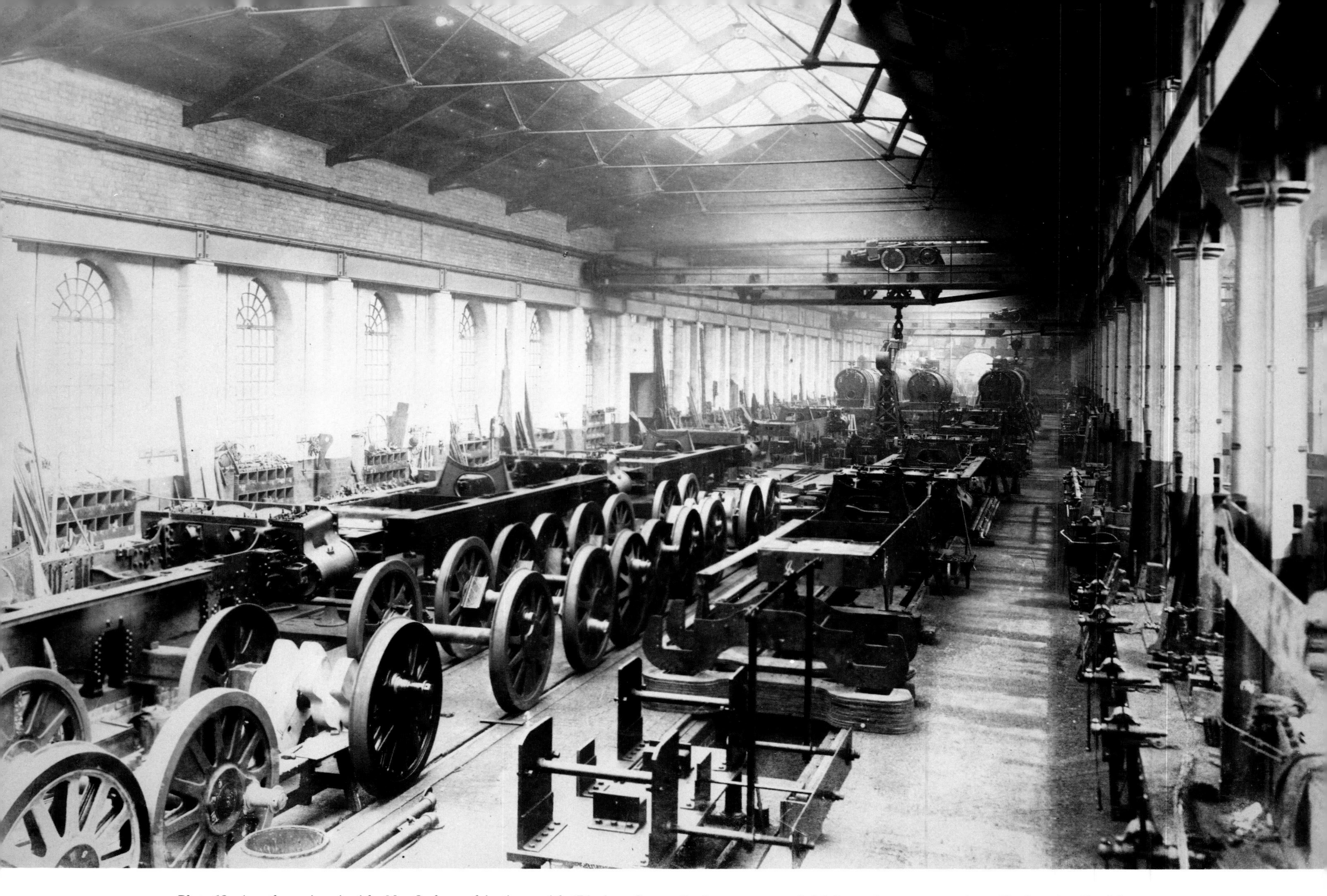

Plate 68: Another view inside No. 8 shop, this time with 'B' class four-cylinder compound 0-8-0s under construction. Similar detail of frame construction can be seen. In the right foreground are frame plates for bogies.

Plate 69: No. 9 erecting shop with Whale 'Precursor Tanks' under construction, circa May 1906. The lights are electric. Heating is provided by warm air through the 'grids', as they are known, in the floor. Incorporated as part of the 'grids' were the rails of the narrow gauge, a short length of track being installed to serve the shop. The cab side-sheet, lower right, is lying on a narrow gauge wagon. This was Mr Webb's last erecting shop. It was built away from, and to the west of, the main complex of buildings at the Steel Works.

The Narrow Gauge Railway System

Plate 70: For internal transport within and between the various shops, the Works was served by an 18in. gauge railway system, which was laid down originally by John Ramsbottom in the early 1860s. The first engine he built was *Tiny*, seen here in a quite early view, photographed perhaps in the 1880s.

Plate 71: Eventually, four other engines like *Tiny* were built, *Pet, Nipper, Topsy* and *Midge*. This view shows *Nipper,* on 25th April 1900. Although from the paintwork the engine seems to have been in service some while since its last overhaul, it is still smartly kept. It seems quite likely that at this stage each engine had its own regular driver, who doubtless kept it in first-class condition.

Plate 72: Pet, with wagons front and rear, somewhere in the vicinity of the foundry, circa 1920.

Plate 73: Two somewhat battered and unidentifiable members of the class, circa 1920, also by the foundry.

Plate 74: During 1875/6 Mr Webb ordered two more narrow gauge engines, which were named *Billy* and *Dickie. Billy* is seen here by the Old Works in the early 1890s. On the left is a Trevithick 'Crewe Goods' 2-4-0.

Plate 75: In the late 1890s, an experiment was carried out to test the idea of hauling canal barges by means of 18in. gauge engines working along the towpath. This is the scene at Cholmondston, looking towards Barbridge, on the Middlewich branch of the Ellesmere & Chester canal, with *Dickie* pulling six barges on about a mile of track. F. W. Webb himself is on the left.

Plates 76 & 77 (left): A somewhat battered and weary-looking *Billy* in the 1920s.

Plate 79 (above right): The narrow gauge railway not only served various parts of the Works but also linked the Old Works with Crewe Station. In this way parts needed urgently anywhere on the company's system could be taken to the station and despatched by passenger or parcel train. The line reached the station by means of a suspension bridge across the tracks of the north junction to the footbridge at the north end of the platforms. This bridge is often referred to as the 'spider bridge', presumably because of the way its supports straddled the tracks beneath it, but according to Brian Reed, it was also known as the 'midge bridge'. This name was presumably derived from the fact that *Midge* worked at the Old Works and so regularly appeared on the bridge. Here, *Midge* is seen at the station end of the bridge. It is obviously waiting while the wagon it has propelled is unloaded.

Plate 80 (below right): A view looking along the 'spider' or 'midge bridge' towards the Old Works, on 14th July 1906, and showing the way the new Crewe North Junction signal cabin was built round the narrow gauge track.

Plate 78: When the Works was reorganised by the LMS in the 1930s, the narrow gauge system was done away with in the Old Works and Steel Works except for a new layout in the steel plant itself. This was worked by *Billy* until the end of 1930, when a 20hp Hudswell Clarke diesel named *Crewe* took over until the closure of the steel plant in 1932. *Crewe,* numbered 5519 and complete with proper LNWR-style chimney, is seen here on this duty. Either side of it are two of the wagons which are thought to have been specially made for use in the Steel Works. They were one-piece iron castings and so were extremely strong, and able to take the weight of steel ingots.

Tender Shop

Plate 81: With paintwork clean but somewhat battered, *Tiny* stands in the tender shop, in the 1890s. On the right is a wooden tender frame, and beyond it one of the standard U-shaped tanks.

Plate 82: A completed, 1,800 gallon tender in the tender shop, probably photographed on the same occasion as the previous picture. The inside of the tank appears to be galvanised, that process being widely used in the Works as a means of protecting iron and steel from rust.

The Royal Visit

On 21st April 1913, King George V and Queen Mary made an official visit to Crewe Works. The event was well covered by the official photographer and a very fine souvenir album was produced. A few of these albums have survived to this day and many of the photographs which follow are taken from one of them.

Plate 83: The Royal Party travelled to Crewe in the Royal Train, hauled by two 'George the Fifth' class engines, No. 2663 *George the Fifth* and No. 5000 *Coronation.* At Crewe Station the King and Queen were welcomed by the mayor of Crewe, who is seen here reading the loyal address to them on arrival.

THIS TABLET COMMEMORATES THE VISIT OF THEIR MAJESTIES KING GEORGE V AND QUEEN MARY TO CREWE WORKS ON APRIL 21ST 1913, FREDERICK MANNING, A SIGNALMAN IN CHARGE OF THIS BOX, BEING MAYOR OF CREWE. ON BEHALF OF HIS FELLOW TOWNSMEN HE RECEIVED THEIR MAJESTIES AND PRESENTED THEM WITH AN ADDRESS ON THEIR ARRIVAL AT CREWE STATION.

Plate 84: The mayor was a signalman in Crewe North Junction box. His part in the visit was recorded by this commemorative tablet placed in the box itself.

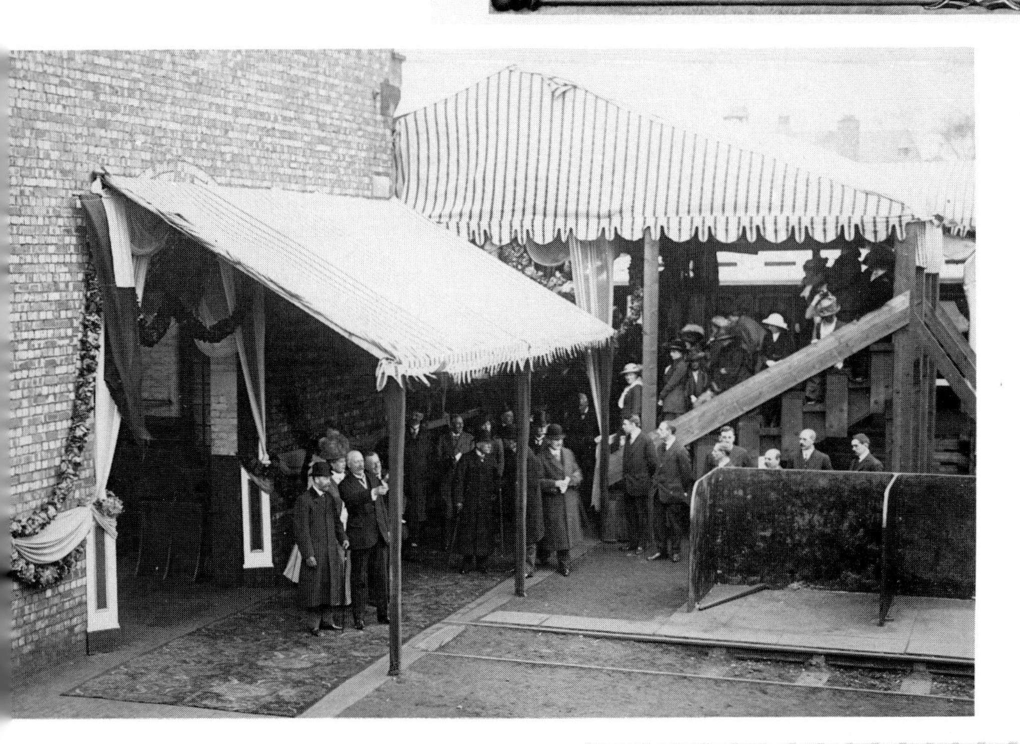

Plate 85: The Royal Train then entered the Works and proceeded to the far west end by No. 9 erecting shop. In the yard were several exhibits, including historic coaches and the first of the 'Claughton' class, No. 2222 *Sir Gilbert Claughton,* recently completed. Here the party is seen outside the machine shop.

Plate 86: Another view of the Royal Party outside the machine shop. King George V is on the left and next to him is C. J. Bowen Cooke, who is pointing something out. Next is Queen Mary, accompanied by Sir Gilbert Claughton, the LNWR Company Chairman.

Plate 87: C. J. Bowen Cooke escorting the Royal Party on board the immaculately prepared 'cab' which took them on their tour from the west end to the Old Works. Normally, of course, these 'cabs' were used to provide a regular service from one end of the Works to the other, and between the Works and station.

Plate 88: The Royal Party, having completed their tour, inspecting a parade of veterans while proceeding to their cars. In the background is the Old Works.

Plate 89: The second of the 'cabs' in the train. Its postillion is obviously very proud of his situation.

Plate 90: The drawing office in the General Offices, where hundreds of Crewe engines and other products were designed.

Plate 91: The same drawing office was used for a celebration dinner in honour of the Royal visit. Its somewhat austere appearance has been transformed for the occasion. On the tables can be seen specially produced tins of cigarettes commemorating the event, one of which survives in a private collection.

Plate 92: An exhibit in the points and crossings shop, showing the development of permanent way. On the left is a stack of new rails for a particular job, each one being numbered on its end. Doubtless, they will shortly be loaded into one of the wagons behind, to be transported to the site.

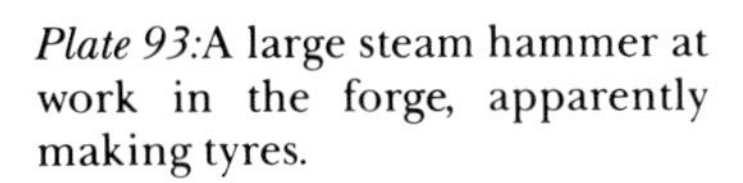

Plate 93: A large steam hammer at work in the forge, apparently making tyres.

Plate 94: Older steam hammers in the forge at the Old Works.

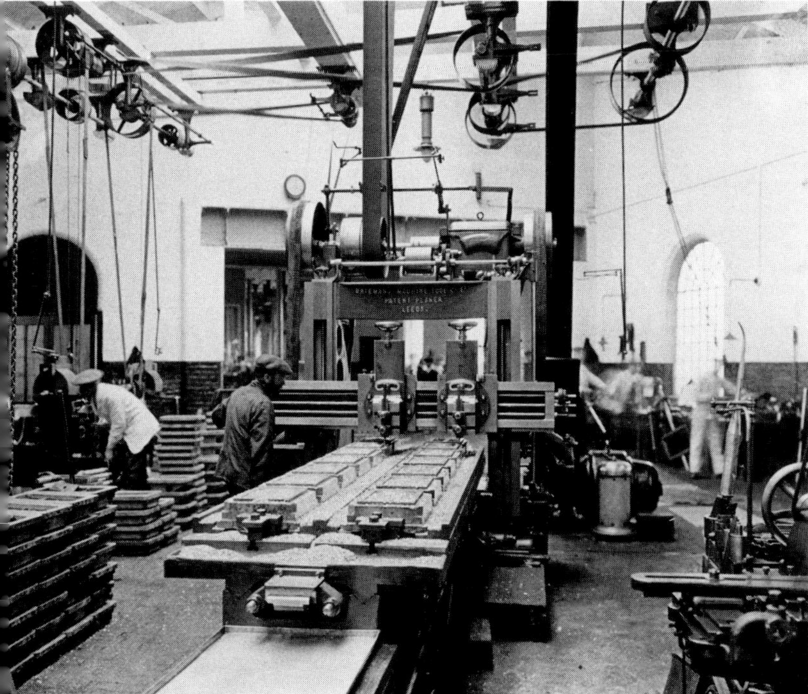

Plate 95: Slide valves being machined on a planer.

Plate 96: Valve gear for a 'Claughton', set out on display in the fitting shop.

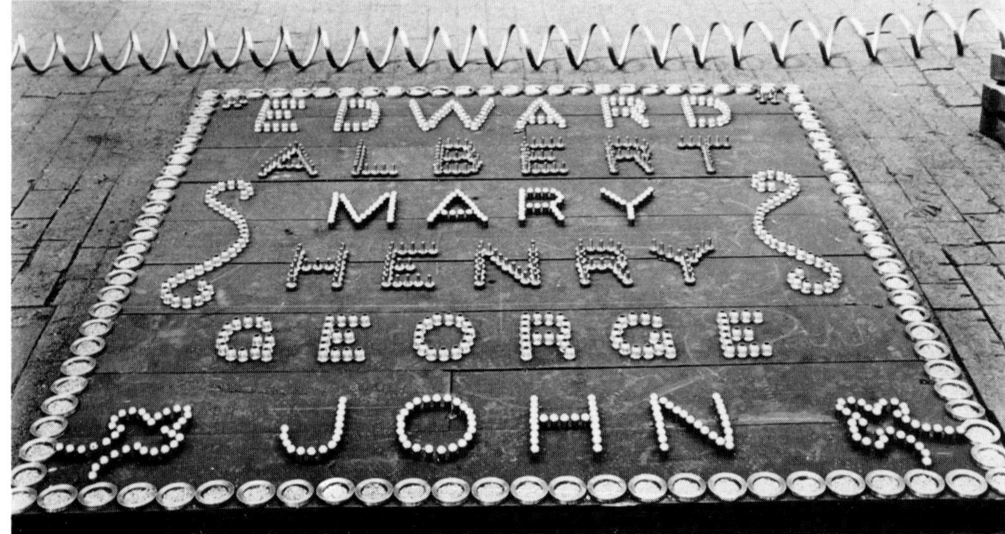

Plates 97-99 (left) & 100 (above right): Four demonstrations of loyalty, made up of items manufactured in the Works.

Plate 101 (below): Pouring molten metal in the foundry, probably iron, although there were also brass and steel foundries.

Plate 102: A tyre-making machine in the tyre mill.

Plate 103: The rail mill. An ingot is being passed through the rollers.

Plate 104: The boiler shop. On the right is a punch for punching holes in plate. Its flywheel is encased in a protective cover.

Plate 105: Precisely what is happening here is uncertain although it is perhaps the end of a tube being shaped in the tube shop. There can be no doubt, however, that the method would not be approved by the factory inspectorate today.

Plate 106: A smith pauses from his task in the Old Works.

Plates 108 & 109 (right): Two views inside No. 9 erecting shop. *Plate 108:* 'George the Fifth' class 4-4-0s under construction. One of the class was named *Loyalty* in honour of the occasion. The men appear to be working naturally, but in fact are carefully holding their poses. With their bowler hats, dark blue suits, white shirts and ties, and highly-polished shoes, the two foremen make a particularly fine sight.

Plate 107: A wheel lathe. The tyres are being turned on driving wheels with large bosses, of the type fitted to many express passenger engines, such as the 'George the Fifths'. The pockets formed on the inside of the boss to take balance weights can be clearly seen.

Crewe Economy

The LNWR and Crewe Works were justifiably renowned for their economical management, and these photographs are good examples of this, since they illustrate the use of old Southern Division engine tender frames for other purposes.

Plate 110: The first mobile electric power unit, or dynamo car, built at the Works, and photographed on 18th May 1896.

Plate 111: A tender frame converted to carry engine boilers.

Plate 112: Two tender frames adapted for transporting rails, circa 1885. The legend on the left reads, 'When unloaded to be returned to Crewe Steel Works'.

Plate 113: Two tender frames adapted for use as a well wagon.

War Work

During World War I, the Works turned over a large proportion of its capacity to war work, so much so that orders for locomotives had to be placed with outside firms, the first time this had occurred since the 1860s. The part played in the war effort by the Works was thoroughly described in *Deeds of a Great Railway* by G. R. S. Darroch. These three views show some of the items produced in that period.

Plate 114 (left): An armoured train for coastal defence, posed with officials on 26th December 1914. In addition to the guns at either end, the train carried riflemen who could fire through slots in the sides of the vehicles, and there were other large guns which fired through portholes (behind where the officials are standing). Motive power is a Great Northern Railway 0-6-2 tank engine. Behind the engine is the stores, the building on the left is the signal shop and, to the right, the tracks lead to the paint shop. A later armoured train, No. 2, was closely similar, except that the tank engine also had a tender, presumably to increase its range.

Plate 115 (left): A Crewe tractor, converted from a Ford motor car, for use on narrow gauge track behind the front line in France. One of its advantages was that it could be safely used at night, whereas a steam engine would give away its position with sparks from the chimney and the glare from the firebox. The photograph is taken at the traditional spot for locomotives, with the gardens of Chester Place in the background.

Plate 116 (above): When required, the road wheels of the Crewe tractor could be removed, and the rail chassis and wheels, carried on the platform, could be fitted.

Plate 117: The Works fire brigade, grouped about their appliance in October 1883. With such beards, it is to be hoped that some them did not get too near a fire.

Plate 118: A hand-powered fire-fighting pump, sometime in the mid-1890s. In the background is one of the company residences for its officers. The gate on the right provided direct access to the Works.

Plate 119: The Works fire brigade in 1925 — the building appears to be the same as that in *Plate 117.*

The Railway and the Town

The town of Crewe owed its origins to the decision by the Grand Junction Railway to transfer its engine Works from Edge Hill to a new site near Crewe Station, and consequently the railway company naturally dominated the life of the town for many years. These pictures show some of the prominent buildings in the town for which the railway was responsible.

Plate 120: Christ Church, which was built by the Grand Junction Railway, for the benefit of its employees and for the inhabitants of Crewe in general. In 1985 the roof was removed, and the area inside the walls made into a garden. The main tower and the tower on the left still stand, as does one of the walls.

CREWE ARMS HOTEL

EUSTON
COFFEE
EUSTON
TAVERN
PARCELS

Plate 121 (left): The Crewe Arms Hotel at around the turn of the century. The exterior is, fortunately, little changed today.

Plate 122 (below left): The Mechanics Institute, founded in 1845. The institute provided a library, reading room and evening classes for the town. The main entrance is on the right, and leads directly to the social club and ballroom upstairs (the latter being run about 1920 by one Rattigan, who worked at the North Shed). On the top floor were the company's laboratories, where, for instance, water analysis was carried out. On the left is Earle Street, leading to Earle Street bridge over the main line. A fine example of an LNWR horse-drawn parcels van is standing in Earle Street. The road surface seems to be crushed stone, well-rolled and cambered for drainage, tarmac not then having been invented; cobble stones are laid at pedestrian crossing places, presumably as being better in wet weather. The glass globes of the street lights would not last long today. The building is now demolished and the site is part of the square between the Market Hall and the Public Library.

Plate 123 (right): Occupying the near corner of the Mechanics Institute in the previous picture is the Euston Coffee Tavern, for which this is the entry in *Eardley's Crewe Almanack.*

"EUSTON"

COFFEE TAVERN

(Adjoining the Mechanics' Institution,)

PRINCE ALBERT St. and EARLE St.;

WEST WING, GODDARD St., WEST St.

(Adjoining the BRANCH READING ROOM, Mechanics' Institution,)

CREWE.

Tea, Coffee, and Cocoa, 1d. per cup.
Tea, specially made, 3d. per small pot.
Aerated Waters, Horehound Beer, &c., 1d. per bottle.
All kinds of Light Refreshments.
Hot Dinners Daily, Chops and Steaks.
Soup Daily; per basin, 2d. Birch's Eccles Cakes.
Melton Mowbray Pies, fresh Daily.
Bovril, served hot.

A First-class Commercial Room.

SPECIAL ROOM FOR LADIES.

Lavatories—No Additional Charge.

☞ RECEIVING OFFICE FOR PARCELS. LEFT LUGGAGE OFFICE.

CYCLES PUT UP.

Refreshment Checks for Distribution 2/- each Book, containing one dozen.

Plate 124 (below): The Mechanics Institute, from the other end of Earle Street. This street, of course, was named after Sir Hardman Earle, a Director of the LNWR, and previously of the Grand Junction and Liverpool & Manchester railways.

Plate 125: The electrical laboratory in the Mechanics Institute, on 18th July 1907.

Plate 126: The art room in the Mechanics Institute, on 17th July 1907.

Plate 127: The Webb Orphanage, which was built with money left for that purpose in F. W. Webb's will, and was completed in 1911. It is now the BR Technical Training College.

Plate 128: Crewe Memorial Cottage Hospital, on 13th September 1900. It was opened by the Earl of Crewe on 7th August 1895. F. W. Webb is standing on the right of the door, behind the woman in the straw hat.

Plate 129: To mark both the Golden Jubilee of Queen Victoria and the fiftieth anniversary of the coming of the railway to Crewe, the LNWR presented Queen's Park to the town. It was dedicated to the public by Sir Richard Moon, on 4th July 1887, and was opened on 9th June 1888.

Plate 130: It is not certain, but seems quite likely, that this bonfire was part of the celebrations of Queen Victoria's Diamond Jubilee in 1897. The location is the ash tip, south of the Chester line near the Carriage Works, on which the slag from the Steel Works was dumped daily. It was brought across the Eagle Bridge by one of the Works shunters — one can be seen on the right. The building on the left is the boiler shop and the left-hand chimney is that of the brick kiln.

The Signal Shop

Signalling equipment was made at Crewe from 1874, although photographs inside the signal shop are rare. These two views were taken at widely differing periods.

Plate 131: A Webb frame being constructed in the 1890s.

Plate 132: The lever frame being prepared for the new Stafford No. 5 box, which was opened in 1952 and is still in use. At this period, the Old Works was used mainly for signal equipment, points and crossings, and lamps.

The Paint Shop

Plate 133 (left): Inside the paint shop, circa 1894. In the centre is the front end of an 'A' class three-cylinder compound 0-8-0, and on the right is the first of the '7ft. 6in. Singles', No. 184 *Problem.*

Plate 135 (right): Painters at work on new LMS 'Jubilee' class 4-6-0s on 14th September 1934. On the left is No. 5624, and in the centre No. 5625; they were later named *St. Helena* and *Sarawak* respectively. At one time, it was said that the cost of painting an engine was greater than that of erecting it, and engines stayed in the paint shop for four weeks or more. However, as the process of painting was speeded up with the introduction of new methods, engines stayed in the shop for a much shorter time, and so by the 1930s only about six of the sixteen roads were usually taken up by engines being painted. Some of the spare roads were then used for storing other engines such as the preserved *Cornwall,* seen here on the right. Gas lights now have mantles but no globes.

Plate 134 (below): The paint shop on the occasion of the Royal Visit, on 21st April 1913. On the right is 'Precursor' No. 2166 *Shooting Star,* newly rebuilt with 'George the Fifth' superheated boiler and cylinders. It is undergoing the laborious process of stopping, filling and rubbing down, several times, preparatory to painting. In the centre is 'George the Fifth' class No. 82 *Charles Dickens,* whose painting appears to be almost complete, and on the left are other newly-painted engines.

Plate 136 (left): Two engines stored in the paint shop on 14th June 1936 were Nos. 3014 and 3015, the cut-down '2ft. 6in. Shunters', which from their introduction in the early 1880s had worked at the Steel Works, supplying the furnaces. When steel production ceased in 1932, they were no longer needed.

Plate 137 (above): In LNWR days many engines were photographed by the official photographer in a location specially arranged for that purpose on the south side of the paint shop. The engine was painted with special paint, which gave it an ideal matt surface for photography, free from the awkward reflections produced by the normal high-gloss finish, the lining was reproduced exactly as in the standard livery, and the engine was seen against a perfectly clear background. This picture shows how that background was achieved, by means of a canvas screen erected behind the engine, which in this case is the first of the 0-4-2 'Bissell Tanks'. A clear background could also be obtained by painting out on the glass negative, but the canvas screen simplified this task greatly and probably made it unnecessary. It is not unknown for engine parts such as lamp irons and cab handrails to be painted out along with the background in some photographs.

Plate 138 (below): An unusual photograph, taken for publicity purposes on 28th October 1897, showing the materials used in the manufacture of one of Mr Webb's three-cylinder compound 'Coal Engines' — No. 50 was the first of the class and was completed in 1893. As usual, the background has been painted out.

Plate 139 (above): In LMS days, official photographs of engines were still produced with a clear background. This 1933 view, however, of the first LMS Pacific, No. 6200, later named *The Princess Royal*, shows the whole of the background, both the wall of the paint shop and the wooden framework for supporting the canvas screen. The chimney on the left is above the boiler house, which heated the paint shop, so as to help to dry the paint, and also provided hot water for the painters. The hottest pit was No. 16, nearest the boiler, and the coolest, No. 1.

Plate 140 (above): Three of the most striking engines ever to be produced at Crewe Works, LMS streamlined 'Coronation' class Pacifics Nos. 6220 *Coronation*, 6221 *Queen Elizabeth* and 6222 *Queen Mary*, posed for the official photographer outside the paint shop in 1937. They were painted in 'coronation blue' with silver stripes and were built to work the 'Coronation Scot' train between London and Glasgow. For many enthusiasts, these engines represented the highest achievement, both aesthetically and mechanically, of British locomotive engineering.

Plate 141 (below): A Webb '5ft. 6in. 2-4-2 Tank', BR No. 46680, outside the paint shop on 11th February 1951. The numbers of the various pits in the shop are shown above the doors, while between the doors are the drain pipes from the north-light roof.

Plate 142: The LMS 'Garratts', built by Beyer-Peacock, were allocated to Crewe Works for repair, and were very unpopular with the men who had to work on them, although whether this was just because they were different from other engines dealt with at Crewe is uncertain. Here, 'Garratt' No. 47967 stands outside the paint shop on 5th December 1948. It is in the early BR livery, plain black with no crest, and with 'BRITISH RAILWAYS' in full, and the number, in straw.

Plate 143: The 'Garratts' were largely replaced by the BR Standard 9F 2-10-0s, many of which were built and overhauled at Crewe. Here, No. 92047 stands outside the paint shop alongside Stanier Class 5 No. 44708, on 13th October 1963.

From the Paint Shop to the West End

Plate 144: The scene looking west from roughly where the tracks from Flag Lane bridge join those from the paint shop, on 8th March 1925. The picture is a composite made by joining two photographs together. On the right are tenders awaiting attention, and in front of them are tanks of various sorts, some being saddle tanks and others being the tanks which once held oil on tenders, during the trials with oil-burning.

Plate 145: Alongside the wheel shop was built a new weigh-house to replace the one at the Old Works. It is seen here when still quite new about 1960, with Class 5 No. 44805 about to enter. This weigh-house was still in use early in 1986, but was about to be replaced by an electronic installation.

Plate 147 (below): The Goddard Street entrance, also in LMS days.

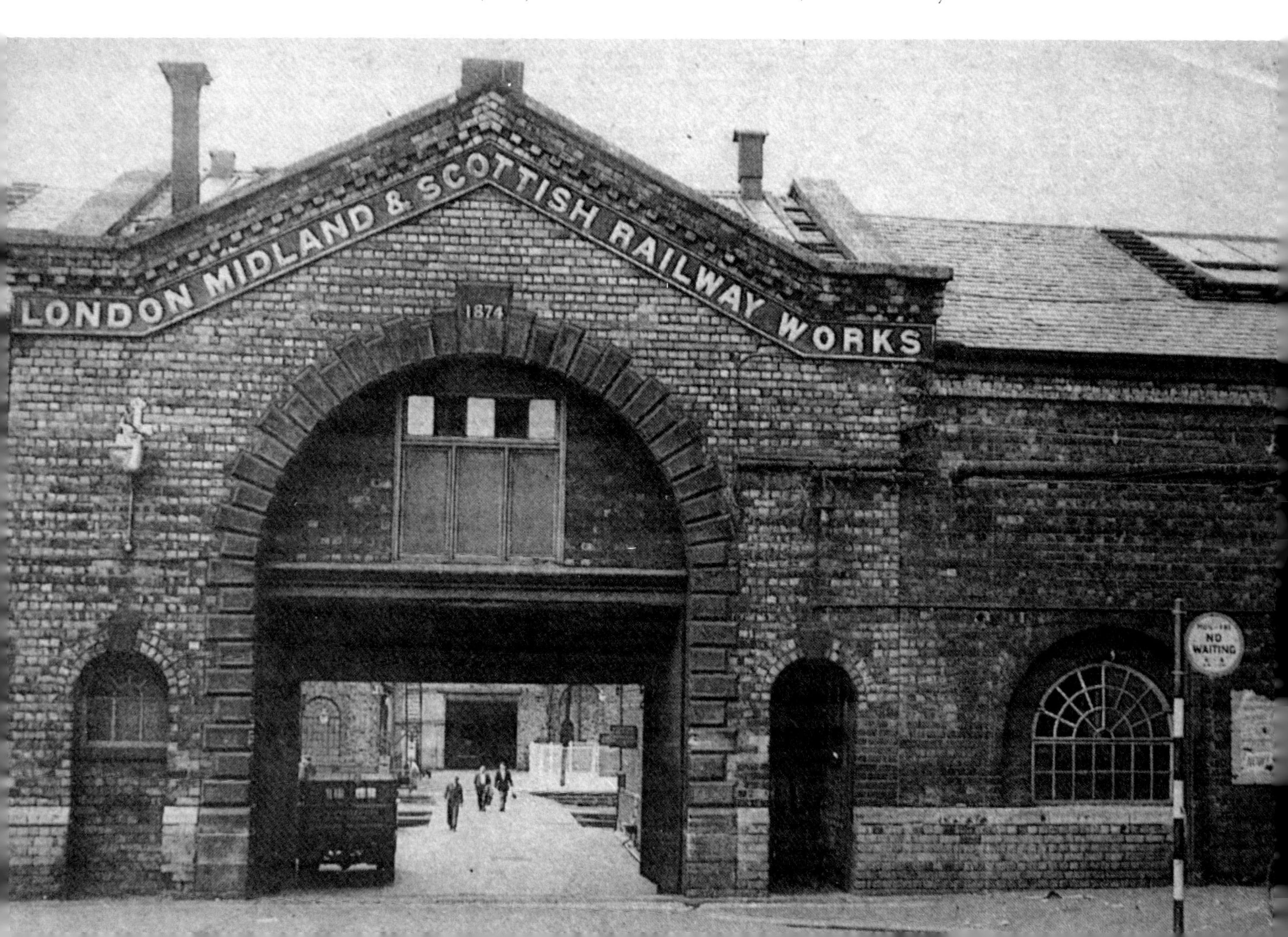

Plate 146 (left): Ramsbottom '4ft. Shunter' No. 3009 on one of its regular trips with the 'cab' from the Old Works to the west end. The bowler-hatted figure is a pay clerk, who is either going to deliver the pay to the men in one of the shops, or to the pay station near the iron foundry. In and by the 'cab' are three more pay clerks who are passing the time of day while waiting for him. The picture dates from early LMS days.

Plate 148 (above): A view of the engine stabling roads between the shops, looking east, on 13th March 1927. The engines are mainly ex-LNWR types, but there is also a North Staffordshire 0-6-0 tank on the left, a North London 4-4-0 tank in the centre, and several ROD 2-8-0s on the right.

Plates 149 (above) & 150 (below): Two views of a display of engines arranged for a visit by the Institute of Civil Engineers on 6th June 1928. The engines are, left to right, 'Royal Scot' class 4-6-0 No. 6149 *Lady of the Lake*, 'Rebuilt Claughton' class 4-6-0 No. 5989 *Vindictive*, 'Cauliflower' 0-6-0 No. 8527, '8ft. 6in. Single' No. 3020 *Cornwall*, with polished brass dome, the Trevithick 'Old Crewe' 6ft. Single *Columbine*, and a replica of *Rocket*. In *Plate 150* the building beyond *Columbine* is the iron foundry; to the right of it is the tender shop. The tender numberplate of *Cornwall*, No. 1509, has its figures and border picked out in white, while that of *Columbine*, No. 3001, is black all over. This reflects what seems to have been the normal situation — some were white — the 'standard' style being one or the other, depending on the whim of the painter.

L M S
L M S

No. 10 Erecting Shop

Plate 151 (right): A view of Crewe Works, circa 1905, from the west end, with the back of No. 9 erecting shop on the left, and rows of Webb and Whale engines awaiting attention.

Plate 152 (Below): A view photographed in the late 19th century looking towards the Works and Crewe Station from Merrill's Bridge, which carries West Street over the Chester line. On the extreme left is the coal yard; one of the wagons is lettered 'Florence Colliery'. The circular building with the tall chimney, in the centre, is the brick-making mill, and the two chimneys to the right of it belong to the iron foundry. Alongside the main line is the boiler shop, to its left is the plate stores and flanging shop, and left of that is No. 8 erecting shop. In the foreground on the left is the site of the new erecting shop, No. 10, built in the 1920s. The buildings in the distance on the right are those of the Carriage Works.

Plate 153: Boilers being loaded on to a special wagon by a Ransomes & Rapier steam breakdown crane. Behind is West Street and St Barnabas Church. The date is 22nd April 1912.

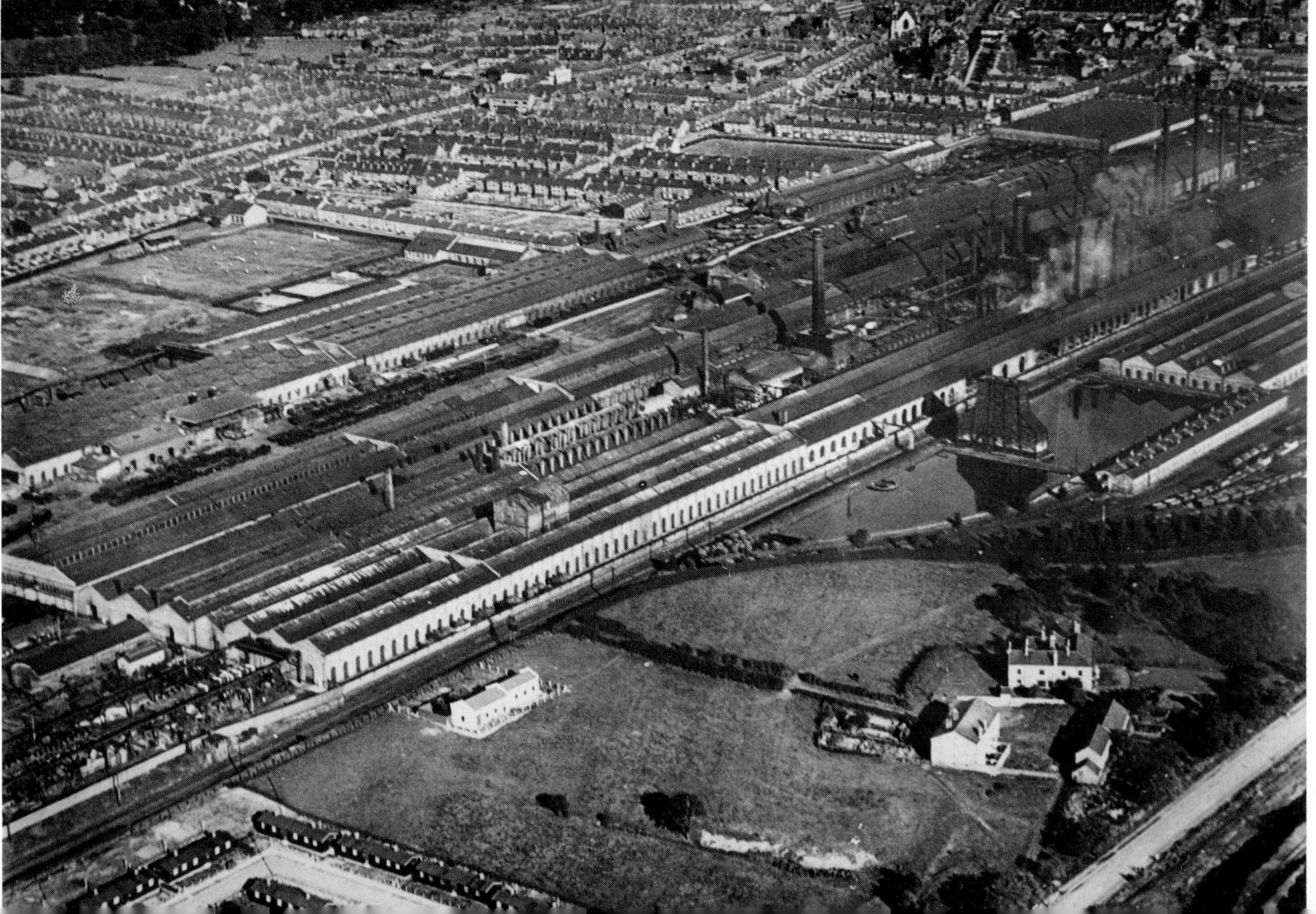

Plate 156 (right): One of the government huts, sometimes referred to as the 'Park Huts', built during World War I.

Plate 154 (left): An aerial view, photographed about 1926 with the new erecting shop, No. 10 shop, nearing completion. Merrill's Bridge is just out of the picture on the left, but the houses of West Street can be seen behind the new shop. On the extreme left, with a low roof, is south shop, which had only 10-ton cranes; the high building nearest the camera is No. 10 shop. Beyond it, and extending slightly more to the east, is No. 9 shop, No. 9 shop arcade, and the machine shop, which were built by Webb shortly before his retirement. In the foreground, south of the Chester line, can be seen some of the government huts erected during World War I to accommodate additional workers employed on the war effort. Beyond the shops is the area where boilers are stored in the open and in the estate beyond that two of the roads are named Bowen Cooke Avenue and Frank Webb Avenue.

Plate 155 (left): A view photographed on the same occasion from roughly the same position, but looking north-east across the Chester line to the main part of the Works. In the centre of the picture is the main complex of shops, with the Steel Works on the right. Beyond are lines of engines awaiting repair and beyond them are more shops, including the tender shop. South of the Chester line, centre right, are the cooling ponds for the rail mill, north of the line, and on the extreme right is the Carriage Works.

Plates 157 & 158 (below): After World War I, a thorough reorganisation and modernisation of Crewe Works took place, of which the construction of the new erecting shop, No. 10, was really only a part. These two diagrams show the arrangement and purpose of the various shops before (Diagram A) and after (Diagram B) the reorganisation.

DIAGRAM A.

1. BRICK MAKING MILL.
2. IRON FOUNDRY.
3. CHAIR FOUNDRY.
4. PATTERN SHOP. & STORES
5. TENDER SHOP.
6. BRASS FOUNDRY.
7. COPPER & TUBE SHOP.
8. SIGNAL SHOP.
9. WHEEL SHOP.
10. NUT & BOLT SHOP.
11. PAINT SHOP.

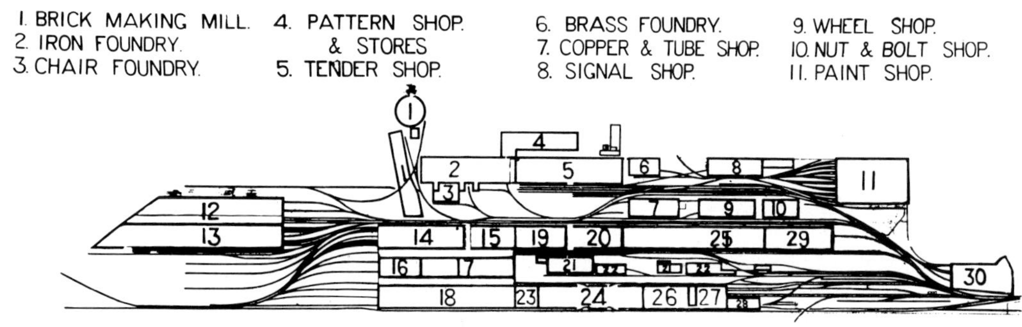

12. MACHINE SHOP.
13. Nº 9 ERECTING SHOP.
14. Nº 8 ERECTING SHOP.
15. BOILER MOUNTING SHOP.
16. PLATE STORES.
17. FLANGING SHOP & ANGLE IRON SMITHY.
18. BOILER SHOP.
19. Nº 6 ERECTING SHOP.
20. Nº 5 ERECTING SHOP.
21. POWER & BOILER HOUSES.
22. GAS PRODUCERS.
23. POINTS & CROSSING SHOP.
24. RAIL MILL.
25. FORGE.
26. 20 TON FURNACES.
27. SPRING MILL.
28. 30 TON FURNACES.
29. STEEL FOUNDRY.
30. STONEYARD.

DIAGRAM B.

1. BRICK MAKING MILL.
2. CHAIR FOUNDRY.
3. 6 TON GANTRY.
4. IRON FOUNDRY.
5. PATTERN SHOP. & STORES.
6. TENDER SHOP.
7. ENGINE STORAGE ROADS.
8. BRASS FOUNDRY.
9. BRASS FINISHING SHOP.
10. COPPER SHOP.
11. WHEEL SHOP.
12. PAINT SHOP.

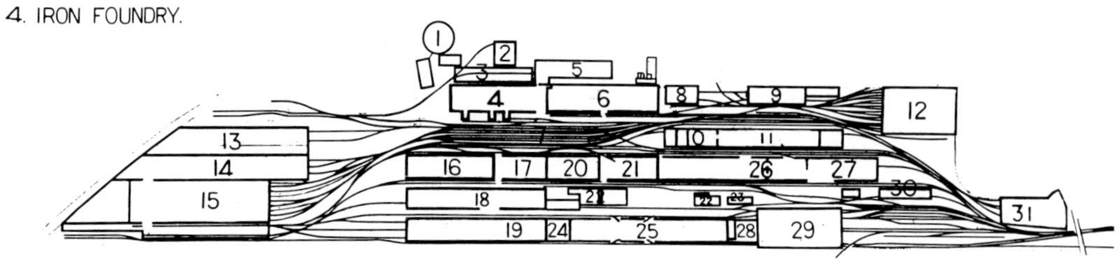

13. MACHINE SHOP.
14. Nº 9 ERECTING SHOP.
15. NEW ERECTING SHOP.
16. FINISHED PART STORES & WELDERS SHOP.
17. MOUNTING SHOP.
18. SMITHY.
19. BOILER REPAIR SHOP.
20. TUBE SHOP.
21. HEAVY MACHINE SHOP.
22. POWER & BOILER HOUSES.
23. GAS PRODUCERS.
24. POINTS & CROSSING SHOP.
25. RAIL MILL.
26. FORGE.
27. STEEL FOUNDRY.
28. SPRING MILL.
29. NEW MELTING FURNACES.
30. INGOT STACKING GANTRY.
31. STONEYARD.

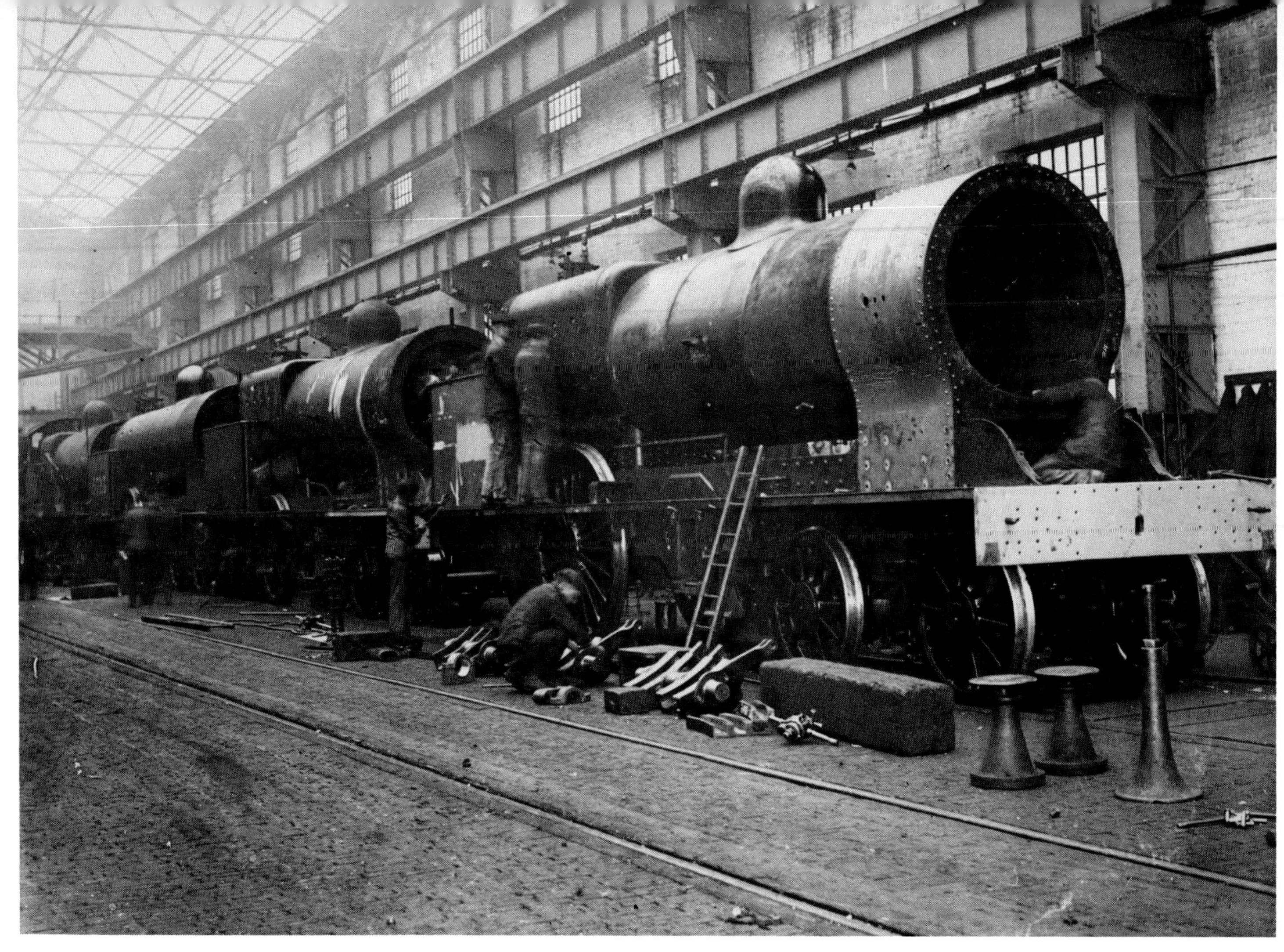

Plate 159: The new erecting shop was designed originally to repair engines on a production-line system known as 'the belts', a whole line of engines being moved forward at fixed intervals as each stage of repair was completed. This early view shows ex-LNWR engines under repair, the one nearest the camera being a 'Precursor'.

Plate 160 (left): The caption on the back of the original print reads, 'applying local heat to the bent frame of an engine, 12th March 1931'. The engine seems to be a Webb 2-4-2 tank, and no doubt its frame would soon be effectively straightened, despite the apparently crude method being used, thanks to the experience of the man doing the job.

Plate 161 (right): In the mid-1930s the Works was extremely busy building engines to Stanier's new designs, two new engines being turned out each week. On the right new three-cylinder 'Jubilee' class 4-6-0s are under construction, while on the left, other classes, including ex-LNWR 'Super Ds' and LMS standard 3F 0-6-0 tanks, are being repaired, on 14th September 1934.

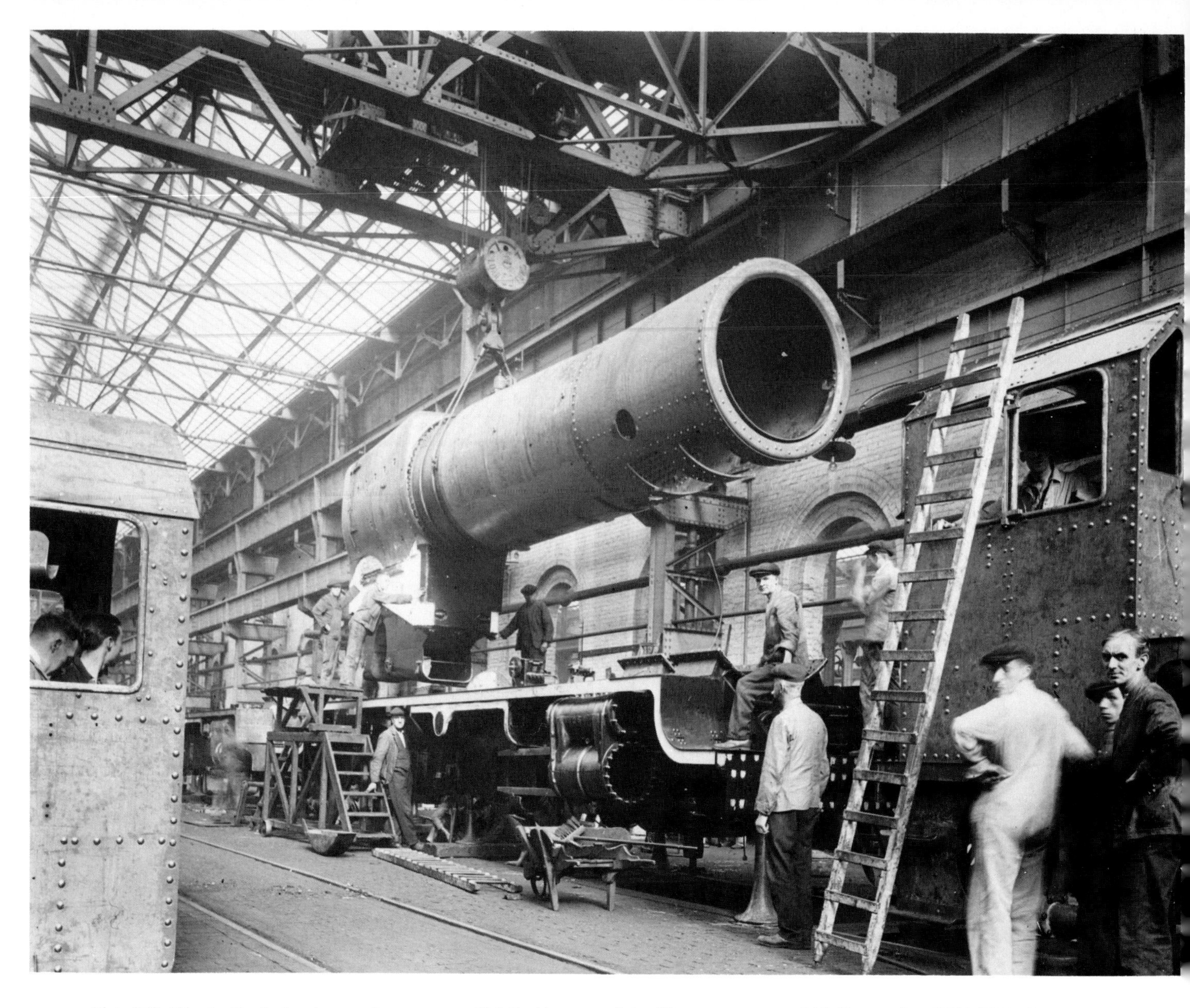

Plate 162: The boiler being lowered on to a new 'Jubilee' by one of the 50-ton cranes, on 14th September 1934. This shop had two crane runs, 10-ton cranes on the lower run and 50-ton on the upper.

Plate 163: Completed 'Jubilees' Nos. 5622 and 5623, later to be named *Nyasaland* and *Palestine* respectively. Beyond them are the two engine units of a 'Garratt'.

Plate 164: No. 5624, later to be named *St. Helena*, outside the shop.

Plate 165: A demonstration of the giant hooks used for lifting engines, in 1931.

Plate 167 (right): The first of the 'Royal Scot' class, No. 6100 *Royal Scot*, under repair on 22nd July 1934.

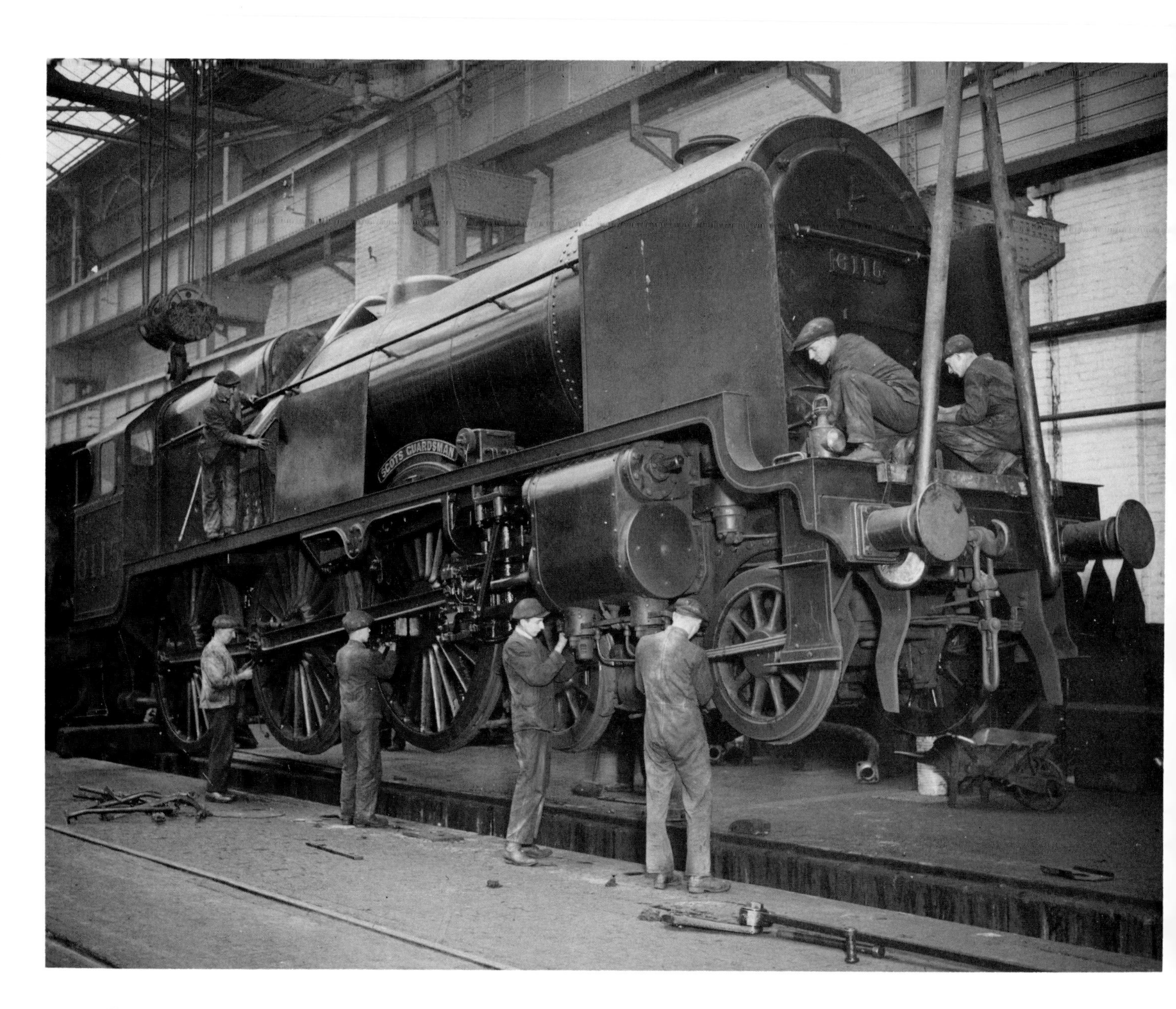

Plate 166 (above): 'Royal Scot' class 4-6-0 No. 6115 *Scots Guardsman* suspended in mid-air while men work on it. In view of the angle of the engine and the positions of some of the men, the photograph seems somewhat artificially posed.

Plate 168 (right): A sign of things to come. One of the pioneer LMS diesel shunters, No. 7073, in the shop for repair on 18th April 1937.

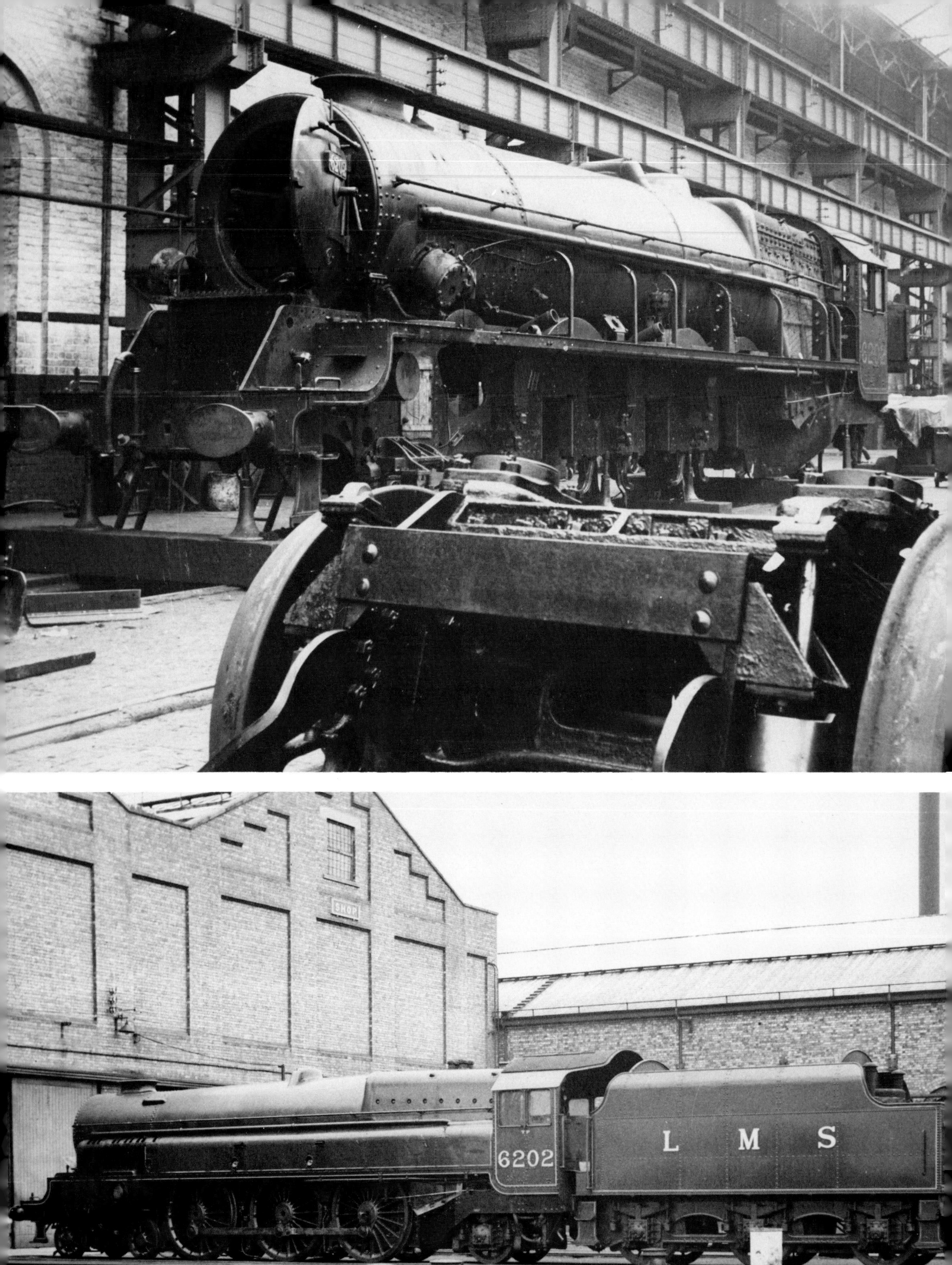
SHOP
6202
L M S

Plate 169 (left): The turbine-driven Stanier Pacific, No. 6202, generally known as 'the turbo', under repair on 14th February 1937, with the casing alongside the boiler removed.

Plate 170 (left): No. 6202 outside the shop on 14th June 1936; behind it is No. 9 Shop.

Plate 171 (above): A general interior view at the west end of No. 10 shop on 3rd March 1935. On the left is 'Cauliflower' 0-6-0 No. 8543; behind it is a 'Garratt'. In the centre is 'Rebuilt Claughton' No. 6013, behind it is 'Super D' No. 9388, and behind that is a 'Cauliflower'. In the foreground is the traverser, while behind the camera is what is now known as 'south shop'.

Plate 172: A Bowen Cooke 'Superheater Tank' under repair, LMS No. 6955. On the left is a 4F 0-6-0, No. 4224, a reminder that although essentially a Derby design, some of this class were built at Crewe as well as being repaired there.

Plate 173: The Earlestown Wagon Works 'Special Tank', *Earlestown* under repair on 14th June 1936.

Plate 174: A fine general view of the shop taken about 1953. 'Rebuilt Scots' No. 46146 *The Rifle Brigade* and No. 46152 *The King's Dragoon Guardsman* and Stanier Pacific No. 46257 *City of Salford* are prominent among other Stanier named engines, Class 5 4-6-0s and 8F 2-8-0s.

Plate 175: Hazeldine & Co.'s stationary engine, built around 1814, which was refurbished and stored in the paint shop.

Plate 176: The celebrated Penydaren locomotive, designed by Richard Trevithick, which in its historic trial of 1804 on the existing tramway at Penydaren Ironworks, South Wales, was the first successful example of steam locomotion on tracks. It hauled 10 tons of iron and 70 men from Penydaren to Abercynon, 9¾ miles, and so won the owner of the ironworks 500 guineas in a bet with another ironmaster. Mr Webb found the engine in South Wales and had it brought to Crewe for restoration, but this photograph is thought to be of a replica.

Plate 177: A publicity photograph taken outside No. 10 shop, in June 1930. On the right is newly-completed LMS 'Crab' No. 13178, which was officially the 6,000th engine built at Crewe Works, while on the left is the Crewe replica of *Rocket*, that had been displayed during the 1913 Royal Visit, and behind it *Columbine*, officially the first engine built at Crewe. The capstan, of course, was used for hauling engines out of the shop.

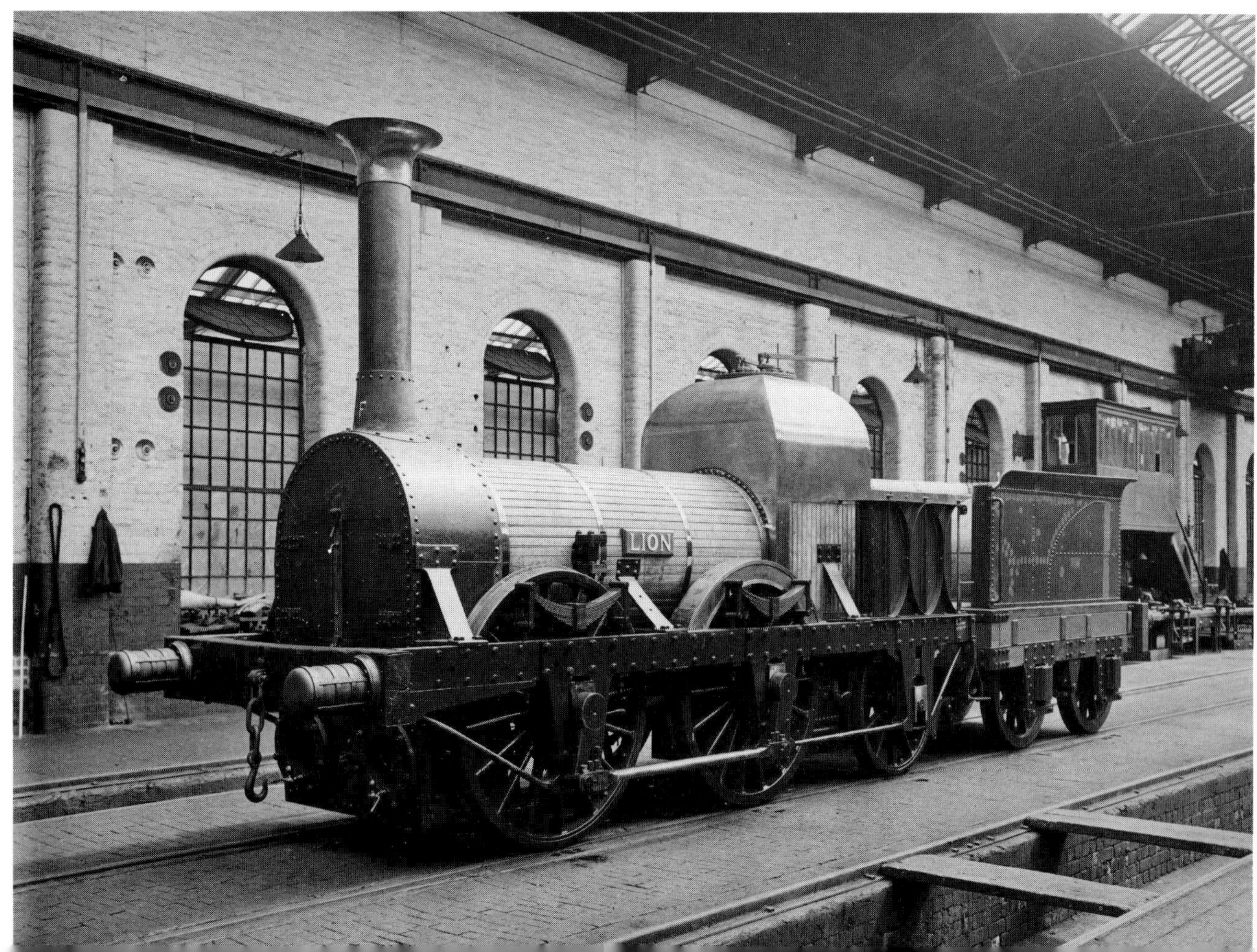
LION

Plate 178 (left): The Liverpool & Manchester Railway 0-4-2 *Lion* undergoing restoration on 18th April 1937. It looks rather strange but the view is of the front of the engine, the chimney being placed on the footplate, where presumably it was out of the way.

Plate 179 (left): The location is No. 9 shop arcade, and *Lion* is in its completed state but before final painting.

Plate 180 (above): Restoration completed, *Lion* stands alongside 'Coronation' class Pacific No. 6229 *Duchess of Hamilton*, which is still in shop grey, having just been pulled out of the erecting shop, out of the picture on the left. Behind the engines is No. 9 shop.

Before and After Overhaul

Plate 181 (above): Engines for overhaul in the Works were sent by their sheds to Crewe South, where they waited until they were brought on to the Works as required. Here, on 18th November 1953, ex-works 'Super D' No. 49104 of 8C shed, Speke Junction, hauls Fairburn 2-6-4 tank No. 42250 and 'Garratt' No. 47979 to the Works for attention. They are about to pass under the footbridge at the north end of the station. The freight avoiding lines are in the cutting behind the coaches.

Plate 182 (above right): 'Patriot' 4-6-0 No. 5527 *Southport* outside the Old Works on 12th June 1938. It has probably only recently been brought on to the Works from the South Shed. Various parts have had the number painted on them in readiness for dismantling.

Plate 183 (below right): LMS Class 5 No. 5235 outside No. 10 Shop, on 16th August 1936. It is one of those built by Armstrong Whitworth but has obviously come into the Works for attention. The LMS livery at this period had plenty of polished metal — rods, tyres, wheel bosses, cylinder covers, smokebox door hinges and straps, and so forth.

5527
L M S
SHOP
L M S
5235
L

Plate 184: 'Patriot' No. 45516 *The Bedfordshire and Hertfordshire Regiment* stands outside the erecting shop on 6th February 1949. This engine was unusual, if not unique, in having BR numbers on LMS maroon paint, which was specially cleaned, and perhaps touched up also, to work a special train for the regiment from Southampton Docks. It appears to have been undergoing repair for that special working when this picture was taken.

Plate 185: 'Royal Scot' class 4-6-0 No. 46127 *Old Contemptibles* on its way after overhaul to the paint shop, on 30th June 1951. The engine has received full undercoat in the erecting shop, but the tender has just had its paintwork cleaned. On the right is the brass shop (the signal shop, before it was moved to Gresty Lane).

Plate 186: 'Coronation' class Pacific No. 46248 *City of Leeds* on its way to the paint shop, on 15th April 1951. It is standing by the brass shop.

Plate 187: Ex-I NWR 'Super D' 0-8-0 No. 9247 in immaculate condition, on 25th September 1938. Clearly, it has just been turned out of the paint shop, which can be seen in the background on the right. It has a 5D shed plate but is believed never to have been allocated to Stoke; perhaps the smokebox door had come from another engine. While these engines were commonly referred to by enginemen and shed staff as 'Super Ds', in the Works they were invariably known as 'four foot threes', from the diameter of their driving wheels, 4ft. 3in.

Plate 188: In LNWR and LMS days it was the practice for engines newly outshopped to be run light to Whitmore on test. Here, on 7th June 1930, 'Claughton' No. 5925 *E. C. Trench*, 'Rebuilt Precursor' No. 5282 *Champion* and 'Royal Scot' No. 6143 *Mail* are arriving at Whitmore on the 'up' slow line. They will stand in the siding adjacent to the 'down' slow line on the right-hand edge of the picture for 1-2 hours before returning to Crewe.

British Railways Standard Engines

Plate 189: Crewe Works was responsible for building all the BR Standard Pacifics, many of the 9F 2-10-0s, and some of the 2-6-2 Class 2 tanks. Here, one of the first batch of 'Britannias', No. 70007 *Coeur de Lion*, is en route in undercoat from the erecting shop to the paint shop, on 15th April 1951. Coupled to it on the right is No. 70008 *Black Prince*.

Plate 190: No. 71000 *Duke of Gloucester*, the only BR Standard Class 8 Pacific, under construction in the erecting shop. On the right is the leading bogie, the ashpan, the footplate floor, and the trailing truck. Beyond, a Stanier Class 5 is receiving a major overhaul.

Plate 191 (above left): The boiler of one of the ten Franco-Crosti Class 9F 2-10-0s being lowered on to the frames.

Plate 192 (below left): The last steam locomotive to be built at Crewe was BR Standard Class 9F 2-10-0 No. 92250, in December 1958. It is seen here on completion before being moved to the paint shop for final painting. Officially, it was the 7,331st steam engine built in the Works.

Plate 193 (above): The frames for No. 92250 in the tender shop.

Plate 194 (below): The completed tender outside the shop.

THE FIRST AND EACH THOUSANDTH LOCOMOTIVE BUILT AT CREWE WORKS.

1845 — 1950

REPRODUCED TO THE SAME SCALE.

1ST. BUILT FEB. 1845
GRAND JUNCTION RLY. Nº 49 "COLUMBINE."
"CREWE" TYPE 2-2-2 PASSENGER TENDER.

1000TH. BUILT DEC. 1866
L.& N.W.R. Nº 613.
DX. CLASS 0-6-0 GOODS TENDER.
PHOTOGRAPH SHOWS No 29 OF SAME CLASS.

2000TH. BUILT MAY 1876
L.& N.W.R. Nº 2233.
2-4-0 4'-6" PASSENGER TANK.

3000TH. BUILT JULY 1887
L.& N.W.R. Nº 600.
3 CYL. COMPOUND 2-2-2-2 PASS. TANK.

4000TH. BUILT MARCH 1900
L.& N.W.R. Nº 1926 "LA FRANCE"
"JUBILEE" CLASS 4 CYL. COMPOUND 4-4-0 PASS. TENDER.

5000TH. BUILT MAY 1911
L.& N.W.R. Nº 1800 "CORONATION"
"GEORGE THE FIFTH" CLASS 4-4-0 PASSENGER TENDER.

6000TH. BUILT JUNE 1930
LM&SR. Nº 13178 (NOW B.R. Nº 42878)
CLASS 5 2-6-0 MIXED TRAFFIC TENDER.

7000TH. BUILT SEP. 1950
B.R. Nº 41272
CLASS 2 2-6-2 MIXED TRAFFIC TANK.

Plate 195: When the 7,000th engine built at Crewe was completed in 1950, this composite view was produced by the publicity department, showing the first engine built at Crewe Works and each 1,000th engine built subsequently. Learned articles by enthusiasts have appeared in journals from time to time, proving the railways' calculations of the identities of these engines to be wrong, but the official versions have gone unamended.

Plate 196: The plaque fitted to the tank side of Ivatt 2-6-2 Class 2 tank No. 41272, completed in September 1950.

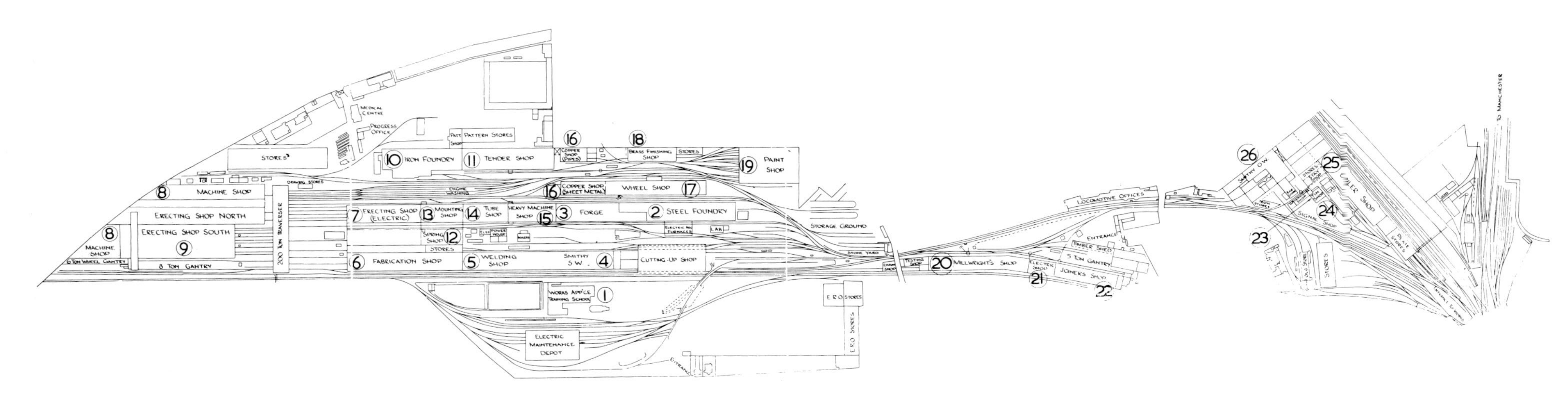

Figure 3: Plan of the Works in the early 1960s when much work was still being done on steam but the transition to other forms of traction had already begun.

1. Works Training School. Apprentices spent the first year of their railway service in the school. All craft grades employed in Crewe Works and in its local departments received classroom and workshop training here.
2. Steel Foundry. The production of steel castings for engine repair and new construction at Crewe, together with a large quantity of castings for other Works and departments. The melting plant had two electric arc furnaces, rated at 3½ and 4 tons respectively, which were installed in 1960.
3. Forge. Heat treatment of locomotive details and production of heavy forgings.
4. Smithy, Steel Works. Manufacture of heavy drop stampings and general smithy work for locomotive and signal details.
5. Welding Shop. The arc welding of assemblies for locomotive construction and repair. The majority of the plates in the assembly were produced by oxy-acetylene cutting machines within the department.
6. Fabrication Shop. Production of large fabrications, primarily the main bodies for new diesel locomotive building.
7. Electric Erecting Shop. All major repairs to electric locomotives, both main line and multiple unit stock.
8. Machine Shop. The main machine and fitting shop in the Works, dealing with all components for new and repaired locomotives. Machine Shop South formed part of the erecting shop and dealt with repairs to wheels, axleboxes, bogies and the like.
9. Erecting Shop. Repairs to all classes of locomotives on a progressive system. New locomotives were also built on similar principles.
10. Iron Foundry. Production of all iron castings required for locomotive work, plant maintenance and outdoor machinery services of the London Midland Region, and also large quantities of signalling components.
11. Tender Shop. Repairs to locomotive tenders.
12. Spring Shop. Repair and renewal of all classes of springs on a modern progressive system.
13. Mounting Shop. Mounting and testing of repaired boilers.
14. Tube Shop. Repair of small and large boiler tubes.
15. Heavy Machine Shop. Machining and assembly of all types of bogies and repairs, and renewals of steam locomotive cylinders.
16. Copper Shop. Production of large sheet plate items such as cabs and aluminium roof fabrications, including roof members. A separate building dealt with copper pipe-work for locomotives.
17. Wheel Shop. Repairs to wheels and axles and manufacture of new wheels and axles for locomotives.
18. Brass Finishing Shop. Machining and fitting of all brass and other non-ferrous details for locomotives.
19. Paint Shop. Painting of new and repaired locomotives.
20. Millwrights and Chain Shop. Maintenance of machinery and plant both for the Works and for outdoor machinery services, and the repair and renewal of lifting tackle.
21. Electric Shop. Maintenace of all electrical equipment and pre-assembly of conduits, cables and instrument panels for locomotives.
22. Joiners Shop. General building maintenance for the whole of the Works and the manufacture of wood packings, food cupboards and such like, for repaired locomotives.
23. Tin and Sheet Metal Shop. General tinware, such as lamps and oil bottles.
24. Signal Shop. Manufacture of all classes of mechanical signalling equipment, and bracket and gantry signals for semaphore and colour light installations.
25. Boiler Shop. General boiler repairs and associated plate work, as on smokeboxes and ashpans.
26. Smithy, Old Works. Manufacture of light drop stampings for locomotives, and for the signal and telecommunications department. It also produced, on suitable forging machines, a large proportion of the black bolts, nuts and rivets used in the Works.

Works Shunting Engines

The following table contains details of the duties of the shunting engines employed in the Works in 1913, and as such is largely valid for the whole of the period 1909 – 20.

No.	*Class*	*Duty*
3001	'4ft. Shunter'	No. 1 'cab' engine
3007	'4ft. Shunter'	Shunting iron foundry and brick yard
3009	'4ft. Shunter'	No. 2 'cab' engine
3084	'4ft. Shunter'	Shunting 30-ton furnaces
3087	'4ft. Shunter'	Shunting 30-ton furnaces
3101	'4ft. Shunter'	Shunting Gas Works
3013	'2ft. 6in. Shunter'	Shunting 20-ton furnaces, day and night shifts
3014	'2ft. 6in. Shunter'	Shunting 20-ton furnaces, day and night shifts
3015	'2ft. 6in. Shunter'	Shunting 20-ton furnaces, day and night shifts
3019	'2ft. 6in. Shunter'	Shunting 20-ton furnaces, day and night shifts
3246	'Crane Shunter'	Shunting wheel shop, paint shop, signal shop and lifting
3247	'Crane Shunter'	Shunting boiler shop, fitting shop, Steel Works and west end bank
3248	'Crane Shunter'	Shunting out-station shop and Steel Works
3249	'Crane Shunter'	Lifting at Steel Works, lifting castings and moulds
3251	'Crane Shunter'	Locomotive stores, fitting shop, shunting and lifting
3252	'Crane Shunter'	Spare for emergencies and when others stopped
3323	'Special Tank'	Shunting at the junction, taking coal to the carriage shops

During the period 1937 – 40 the majority of the Works shunters were '17in. Coal Engines' numbered as follows: 8172, 8227, 8245, 28091, 28100, 28106, 28115 and 28141. Three crane engines were still in use, Nos. 3247-9, and two Ramsbottom '4ft. Shunters'; No. 3009 usually worked the 'cab' and No. 3084 shunted the Gas Works. 'Special Tank' No. 3323 was used to haul dead engines from the Old Works to the west end, and returned with new or newly-overhauled engines from the vacuum pits after steaming tests to the Old Works for weighing.

Except for turns W1 and W3, all Works shunts were manned by Works drivers, who were not allowed beyond the boundaries of the Works. Turn W1 worked two trips daily to and from Basford Hall Sidings. Turn W3 worked one trip to the Grease Works. Its route was from the Works to Salop Goods, where it reversed and ran through the Manchester line tunnel. Both turns W1 and W3 were worked by shed men from the shunting links.

Engines designated for repair in the Works came to Crewe South Shed, where they were held until required. Two or three trips a day were worked between South Shed and the Old Works, each one conveying three or four engines at a time and returning with engines fresh from the Works. The usual engine for this job was a 'Super D' which was working off mileage, or was otherwise unfit for main line work.

Another trip, known locally as 'The Rag Mail', conveyed stores vans between the Works and the station. The engine on this job was one of the three '5ft. 6in. 2-4-2 Tanks' at the North Shed, Nos. 6605, 6711 or 6742.

Plate 197: Mr Webb built some '4ft. Shunters' as 0-4-2 crane tanks, largely for use in the Works. Here No. 3246 appears to be unloading a piece of hydraulic equipment on to a platform barrow at the station, whence it will no doubt be dispatched to its destination. The date is around 1920.

Plate 198: A group of shunters employed in the Works, on 19th December 1911. Their faces reveal a hard way of life, but they are all in full uniform with collars and ties, and clean boots. In the centre of the front row is clearly a man of energy and authority, and the foremen each side of him will obviously stand no nonsense either.

Plate 199: The Works shunting engines always seemed very inferior to the main-line express passenger engines built in the Works or coming in for repair, but they usually outlived their more aristocratic colleagues. Here, in LMS days, Ramsbottom '4ft. Shunter' No. 3009 poses for the camera. It was built in April 1872 and scrapped in October 1946. The cabs provided a service between the Old Works and the west end, and between the Works and station.

Plate 200: '17in. Coal Engine' No. 28115 serving as a Works shunter in November 1938. It has an extra three-link coupling, which was commonly preferred for use in the Works rather than use the screw couplings of engines being hauled. Beyond is a 'Special Tank', almost certainly No. 3323.

Plate 201: Here, ex-LNWR 'Bissell Tank' No. 47865 and an ex-Caledonian 'Pug', No. 56032 stand outside part of the Deviation Works awaiting their next turn of duty, on 12th August 1951. No. 56032 replaced a '4ft. Shunter' as the cab engine.

Plate 202: As the older LNWR engines became worn out and were scrapped, so some Lancashire & Yorkshire types were brought in. Here, in the late 1950s, saddle tank No. 51444 stands by the water tank at the Old Works.

Plate 203: The last LNWR 'Special Tank' to survive at Crewe was No. 3323. This was actually its LNWR duplicate-list number but it retained it throughout the LMS period and until withdrawal in BR days. It was built in May 1878 and scrapped in May 1954. On the left is an LYR 0-6-0 (some 30 – 40 of these were overhauled at Crewe in the early war years, presumably because Horwich was busy on war work), and on the right is a 'Super D' 0-8-0 and a WD 2-8-0. Eventually, standard LMS 3F 0-6-0 tanks were used as Works shunters.

Plate 205 (left): On Sundays it was quite normal for several parties of enthusiasts to tour the Works, and regular guides had the task of shepherding them round and keeping them out of mischief. Here, one of the guides poses for his photograph in the erecting shop.

Plate 204 (left): Visits to the Works by enthusiasts, of course, took place with great regularity, and in great numbers. Nevertheless, it was quite unusual for an enthusiasts' special to run right into the Works itself, as has happened here with the Railway Correspondence & Travel Society's 'East Midlander', hauled by 'Crab' No. 42896 of shed 16D, Mansfield, on 13th October 1963. The paint shop is along the path to the left, and on the extreme left-hand edge of the picture is the water tank in Flag Lane. The engine is standing beside the platform of the old stone yard bank. On the right are two signal boxes, the one nearer the camera having just replaced the older one beyond it.

Scrapping Engines

Plate 206: A somewhat melancholy aspect of the activities of the Works was the scrapping of older engines. Here, in No. 9 shop, on 18th April 1937, Bowen Cooke 'Superheater Tank' No. 6971 is being broken up.

Plate 208 (left): Men engaged on cutting up the boiler of a Webb '17in. Coal Engine' in the early 1950s.

Plate 207 (left): In the same shop, on 13th October 1938, ex-North Staffordshire Railway 0-6-2 tank No. 2242 is broken up.

Plate 209: In BR days part of the old Steel Works was used for breaking up engines. Here, 'Patriot' class 4-6-0 No. 45537 *Private E. Sykes V. C.* awaits attention. Behind it is Stanier 2-6-4 tank No. 42537.

The Last Locomotive Overhauled at Crewe

Plate 210 (above): A rather melancholy event. The last steam engine to be overhauled at Crewe, BR Standard 'Britannia' class 4-6-2 No. 70013 *Oliver Cromwell* is seen with the group of officials and men who worked on it, gathered for the ceremony marking the occasion, on 2nd February 1967. The contrast between the apperance of the men in this picture and those in *plate 198*, taken only 56 years previously, is considerable.

Plate 211 (left): The men crowding round the engine as the mayor leans out of the cab window on the fireman's side. The sadness of the occasion can be seen on the faces of those on the footplate.

A Postscript

by Edward Talbot

With grateful thanks to Roger Bell, Roy Bourne, Bill Broadbent, David R. Brown, Charles Taylor and David Jackson (RBL, RB, WBB, DB, CT and DJ respectively). Any further contributions will be gratefully accepted.

1) As Assistant Works Manager from about 1948 to 1957, my father, Ellis Brown, was allocated West Bank, the house immediately to the west of Chester Place. When he was Manager, from 1960 to 1963 or so, he lived in Ashleigh on the north side of Chester Square. I could see the milepost from the bottom of the garden of West Bank. It was in fact opposite Chester Place, rather than the General Offices. When it was repainted in the 1950s, the original is said to have been stolen and replaced by a totally spurious one. The 'coppice' was reputed to have been formed from spoil when the adjacent joiners', millwrights' and outstation shops were built. (DB)

3) Later there was a gateman in a small hut on the end of the bridge. It must have been the loneliest job in the works. The building which had been a steam shed became the Plate Stores in the 1926 reorganisation. (CT)

5) The Grease Works also provided reclaimed oil from the huge quantity of cotton waste and sweat cloths used as 'wipes' which were washed. It was extracted in large centrifuges before the washing process. It was essential to make sure that all swarf and cuttings were removed from the washed waste. The whole place always smelt of steam, heat and oil. (CT)

The Locomotive Department laundry was also on the Grease Works site. I believe it was the three-storey building with tall chimney just right of centre. Probably they used soap made from processing old grease. I still have some brass plates designed for labelling wicker baskets with 'Wash House Crewe' on one side and the name of a running shed on the other, as well as small copper discs which were used for individual items. (DB)

6) My father began to work here in 1904, on a drill about half way down the middle bay where the belts cross from left to right. (CT)

8) The belts have been joined with leather pieces fastened with copper rivets — the third from the left has four such pieces, one of which is coming adrift. In later years the belts were joined with steel combs clamped to the ends and secured with a steel pin. In 1939 the Machine Shop had three saddlers whose job it was to look after the belts. Powdered resin was poured into the vee between the bottom pulley and the belt to assist grip when the belt was getting slack but was not yet slack enough to justify replacing. The pulleys had a slightly curved profile, being larger at the centre of the face where the belt rode.

The comment about the noise in the shops is inaccurate. Belt drives are in fact a quiet, though not silent, transmission and most of the noise would come from the machines themselves, particularly the gears, and from the slapping of the belts, especially the joins in them, against the wheels, which made a kind of kissing sound. The noise level would not be significantly different from that in a modern machine shop in spite of all the moving parts, though the rumble of the shafting could be heard distinctly on the other side of the walls in West Street and Richard Moon Street. (RB, DB and CT)

11) The start/stop mechanism is not a dog clutch but consists of fast and loose pulleys on the countershaft driving the lathe. The belt driving the countershaft can be seen to pass between the two prongs of a fork mechanism. When the operator pulls the rope, the forks slide and move the belt parallel to the axis of the shaft, giving a smooth start or stop as the belt transfers between the fast and loose pulleys. The pulley at the other end of the belt is of double width to allow for this movement. The fast pulley is keyed to the countershaft while the loose pulley is bushed and runs on the shaft without turning it. (RB)

The layshaft by the top of the right-hand window carries a three-diameter pulley which would be mirrored on the lathe below to enable the speed of the lathe to be altered. In this case the belt was moved by a long piece of wood, about 4in by 4in, the belt being thrown off the larger pulley of the two to give slack, when it tended to flap about, before being led back on to the next one and so on until the right speed was obtained.

12-16) The engine carries number 2153, which was its Crewe Works motion number; the running number, which would have been applied later, was 1140. It was normal Crewe practice for engines which were special in some way, such as those prepared for exhibitions, to carry their motion number. Only when they were put into normal service did they receive their running numbers. The record was broken in 1891 by the Stratford Works of the Great Eastern Railway, which erected an 0-6-0 in 9¾ hours. See *GER Locomotives 1900-1922* by C. Langley Aldrich. (RB)

14) Hand ratchet drills were still used in the 1940s for lacing cylinder bores. (CT) I think the hand-powered ratchet gear would be reaming not drilling the centre horns on the main frame. These holes were mostly pre-drilled as components and then reamed on assembly to accept a light and accurate fit for the rivets. This was still the practice in my days in the Works (1942-5). It would take too long to hand-ratchet drill the holes. (WBB)

18) The weigh house was clearly a natural draught tunnel and the presence of the Iron Bridge did not help. This bridge was railway property and was built to give easy access from the south end of the town to the 'village'. It was closed for one day every year to prevent it becoming a public right of way. (CT)

19) Before the 4-ton drop hammer was moved from the forge in the Old Works in 1940, the vibration it set up could always be felt in the Plaza. (CT) Was this taken from Chester Bridge? The weighbridge building was just to the east of the bridge across or rather under the road from the road entrance to the GO (see Plate No. 21); the Iron Bridge has gone and been replaced by a roadway 'level crossing'. (WBB)

22) The pay was distributed by rail to the shops in one of the 'cabs' depicted in plate 199. (DB)

23-7) Similar decorations were put up for the coronation in 1953. EIIR was placed over the conveniently same number of windows surmounted by a bas relief crown about 8ft high, which was made in the joiners' shop. It was very sad when the General Offices came down. I had a last look round in the 1970s when an electrical firm had a conveyor belt going down the steps to the old line. Frank Webb's office cannot have changed much. On the inside of the bay window were specially fitted drawer units which were probably made of figured walnut, each with a round ivory and ebony handle with inscriptions in 'old English' text, just like old organ stops. The room was dominated by a large table used for poring over drawings rather than for meetings, as the brass paperweights evinced. In a room off was FWW's personal WC with a mahogany-clad low-level cistern. (DB)

24) It must be an early photograph, as the ivy is only just getting hold. On the right are the steps giving direct access to the Chester Bridge end of the GO. (WBB)

25-7) The progress of the ivy is interesting. (WBB)

28-30) As I lived next door, Chester Place was just a wall-scramble away to play with H. P. M. Beames' grandson. I do not remember old man Beames but his son, G. H. P. Beames, who was on the legal side of the LMS/BR lived there with his family for a time. He was a member of the LNWRS until his death in March 1986. It was rather a grim house, slightly enlivened by the model of *Jeanie Deans* in the hallway (is this the model now at Penrhyn Castle?). (DB)

31) The official residences were mostly in Chester Square, Chester Place being the name of the CME's house at the end of Chester Street. (DB)

32) The pierced wall at the bottom of the gardens is very distinctive. The lowest stones are a form of tufa, which seems similar to that found in Via Gellia, Derbyshire. As the C&HPR was so close, transport to Crewe would not be difficult. Above was a course of old stone sleepers and then the brickwork. The wall postdates West Bank and Deva House, which were built in the 1860s, and was put up when the General Offices were built in 1878. From 1947 the wall carried a copper pipe supplying oxygen from tanks at the Old Works to the Steel Works. Until then oxygen had come in by rail and the first cut from the daily trip had been the 'oxo' for the welding shop. After this it came by road. The gates leading to the houses were surmounted by a light over the gate and complemented with one on a post halfway up the garden, operated by two-way switches from both ends. The Grove and Windycote (both of which are shown in this picture, being a pair of large semis) were built a lot later, and the newness of the wall suggests a further westward extension. This portion was still standing in 1989. (DB and CT)

34) Behind the hedge going upwards from behind the smoke deflector was a path leading to a wicket gate in the tarred board fence by Flag Lane bridge. This gate was opened at start and finish times. (CT)

35) The washout plugs on the firebox have been leaking. (CT) The best locomotive Crewe ever produced! (WBB)

36) A close runner up! (WBB)

39) To the right of the engine is the millwrights shop. (WBB)

41) My father is there somewhere. On the skyline from right to left there is Flag Lane tank, St Mary's Catholic Church, Hightown Congregational Church, possibly Beech Street School, and Hightown Wesleyan and St Paul's Churches. (CT)

42) Strictly, the Catholic church is in St Mary's Street, although the side is in Delamere Street. The circular building in the top right of the picture, with a chimney above it, was the Brick Works. Below it was a canteen, which was later used as a store for brasswork and during the war as the headquarters of the Home Guard. At the bottom on the left, separated from a row of houses by an alley, is the Old Vine Inn. The ground between the houses and the wall of the Works seems to be used for allotments. (CT)

45) Ingots on their way to the rolling mills would have to be re-heated before being rolled. (DJ)

46) This is a carefully posed view showing the different stages in rolling a rail. On the far right is the ingot in the cogger, next to it in the smaller rolls it has been reduced in size to a bloom and on the far left is the rail, more or less finished. In the background are recently rolled, and still hot, rails on the cooling banks. (DJ)

48) Fascinated to see that the melters peering into the furnace have shining boots! (DJ) The furnaces were Siemens Martins open hearth. They were closed in 1932, when Lord Stamp decided steel would be bought in. It was always said that the government would not let the LMS knock them down and in 1940 they were brought back into use. They produced reputedly the most expensive steel in the country, as all raw materials had to be brought into the Works and the 50 and 70-ton ingots had to be transported to private industry rolling mills elsewhere, there no longer being a rolling mill. Two 'Super Ds' used to come in on Saturdays to haul the output to Scotland. (CT and WBB)

54) The boring machines were still in use during the war, although by then moved to what was 5 and 6 Shop. Floor-to-floor time for a pair of cylinders complete was a fortnight. (CT)

55) This is the south bay looking east. In 1926 the far end became the Nut and Bolt Shop.

56) This is the north bay looking east. Later a Tool Stores was put between the two bays half way up the shop.

Figure 2) The map shows the narrow pathway which ran from Chester Square down to the old Chester line immediately to the east of The Grove. It used to be laid with timber segments from the centre of spokeless carriage wheels and was for the benefit of officers living on the north side of Chester Square and in Delamere Street. The map also shows the vicarage of Christ Church (nearly, if not the same, size as Chester Place) on the corner of Delamere Street and Lawrence Street. (DB) The houses between Delamere Street and Chester Street were occupied by firemen, and alarm bells in them were wired to the Deviation gate.

Compton's factory in Bridle Road became the Stationery or ERO Stores. Right at the west end was a coal merchant's yard. All his stock came in on the Works trip, until that very cold winter in 1940 when he began to receive empty or almost empty wagons, but that is another story. (CT)

59) This is the Old Works boiler shop. The boilers for the 4-6-2s were so long that there was insufficient head room for the crane, so part of the roof was made moveable and a crane put outside. (CT)

66) After 1926 this became the finished work stores. (CT)

69) The warm air came from steam pipes under the grids, which extended through the machine shop to No. 10 shop. (CT)

75) What a man! (WBB)

80) In my spotting days, 1933-8, when things were quiet it was possible to sneak along the bridge to get a good view of Crewe North. Nobody objected, provided that you were alone and did not stay too long. There was a rumour that if your father worked for the company and you were caught trespassing, he would be sacked. No one put it to the test. (CT)

91) This view shows the table of the officers and directors. Opposite second from the left is Guy Calthrop; fourth from the left is Robert Turnbull. Near side third from the camera is probably Sir Frank Ree, fourth E. C. Trench and seventh, leaning back, Sir Gilbert Claughton. (ET and RBL)

101) Almost certainly, the iron foundry. Looks like a row of chairs being cast. (WBB)

105) There was a similar stone in No. 9 shop in later years but the man sat astride a plank suspended by rope from a girder at the back end and the workpiece was put at the front end. The man's weight applied the required pressure. The stone revolved away from the man, lubrication was by water and the debris was caught in a vertical curved trough behind the stone. (CT) Looks more like the millwrights shop to me. (WBB)

Depicted here is the massive stone grinding wheel that was used as a short cut to making metal bits fit, to avoid the delays of resorting to organising machining or of laborious bench-work with a file as the alternative. When I was an apprentice, my mate would mark off with chalk the shape of how much metal needed to be removed and then despatch me to the old boy sitting on the grinding wheel saddle at the west end of 9 shop, with the strict instruction not to say a word about what was required, but just to hand him the piece to be worked over,

collect it silently after the grinding had been done and return it. Whether he spoke to any family at home we shall never know. One of Crewe's characters! (WBB)
107) The bare stud contacts on the electrical starter can be clearly seen. (CT)
109) The crane has the open commutator and worm drive of the Crewe design. (CT)
110) This was taken in the Deviation Works on the other side of the 'coppice' from the old Chester line.
115) In fact, it is The Grove and Windycote in the background. Probably no photographs were taken with Chester Place in the background. Photographers could only get back far enough by the iron foundry and the weigh-house. I remember G. R. S. Darroch quite well. He lived in a railway officers' house at 44 Delamere Street and had a Bugatti saloon. It was said that he drove it to Italy for servicing and went to London to have his hair cut. He had a fine live-steam model of *Coptic* in his garden, which we rode on, as well as a great bulldog called Jane, which we did not ride on! (DB)
118) Strictly, it should be 'a pair of company residences', Windycote and The Grove.
119) The building is the same. I have a similar photograph of the 1925 group with just the cup and from a slightly different angle. In later years the buildings on the left were used for garaging the Works cars. (DB)
The Works fire buzzer was at the Deviation end and gave four blasts for a company fire; the town buzzer was at the electricity works end and gave three blasts for a town fire. Ne'er the twain did meet! (CT)
120) Even in the 1960s my father still had a say in the appointment of clergy for this church. (DB) It was always said that the church got free gas until 1948. (CT)
121) Below the first floor window on the left front of the building was the entrance to a tunnel leading to the station (it is hidden in the photograph). The pedestrian entrance to this subway is off the foyer of the hotel, inside to the left of the entrance doorway. It is now bricked up but it used to lead to steps up to platforms 5 and 6, and was built for the royal visit, so that their majesties could get off the train from London (interesting bit of signalling to get it across the south junction into platform 6) and walk directly to the hotel instead of having to walk across the road outside the station and down the steps to the hotel. In the event the subway was not used for the occasion of the reception of the royal party, and it was rarely used afterwards, although the hall porters at the Crewe Arms (of whom there were six in the 1940s and early 1950s, when it was still a railway-owned hotel) used to use it for guests' luggage when they were departing by train and had too much to carry up and over. I used it once when loaded with climbing gear, boots, haversack, ice axe, suitcases and so on, on route to a Scottish mountaineering holiday, just to be able to say I had used it. The then Head Porter was Harold. The saddest thing about this subway was that when the great modernisation of the bedrooms took place in the early or middle 1950s, all the copper hot-water cans which were formerly brought to your bedroom morning and evening (a coal fire in the room was 1s extra on the 1949 B&B bill of 12s 6d) were stored in the tunnel. When the railway sold the hotel, the tunnel was bricked up, to seal access to the station. My imagination has it that all this copper memorabilia still lies imprisoned as hidden treasure! (WBB)
122) The windows of the library are to the right of the main door. The library tickets were Edmundson type in various colours to indicate the different classes of subscription. On the left-hand side of the building, beyond the parcels van, was a company parcels office. (CT)
127) During the war there was a National Fire Service station, 41B1Y, behind the left-hand end of the building. (CT)
128) The building has now been demolished and the site used for housing. (DB) The hospital was partly supported by the proceeds from the annual park fete, when all the shops and other departments competed in various contests of dance, music, novelty and so forth, culminating in a grand firework display. (CT)
129) The wooden bridges were replaced by concrete around 1926. The lake is artificial; the Valley Brook or River Waldron passed underneath in a culvert. (CT)
132) Well illustrates the much lighter Midland 'Catch-handle' interlocking design, as compared with the LNWR's massive Webb grab handles. (WBB)
133) Did not look much different when I first went into the shop in 1942 with *Cornwall* and *Hardwicke* in residence. (WBB)
133-5) The paint shop was a peculiar building for a child. It was full of dangerous pits, and there was the cool special light from the north lights, as well as the smell. I was allowed to clamber over *Cornwall*, *Pet* and *Lion* but not the wooden replica of Rocket. I was lucky enough to have a footplate ride on *Lion* when it was overhauled for the film *The Titfield Thunderbolt* in the 1950s. Outside the paint shop, on its long southern elevation, grew masses of blackberries, our main supply point for home. When I became interested in the LNWR *per se*, I fancied that they used the blackberries as a colour reference for the engines! At the east end of the shop there used to be boards painted with the front end stripes for the streamlined 'Coronations' — presumably as a reference — together with a bell or bells. There was direct street access at this point, as there was from Chester Square and by the Pay Office. (DB)
134) There were supposed to be seven coats of primer, undercoat, finish and varnish. In 1951 when 70004 was prepared for the Festival of Britain exhibition at Battersea, the street door was opened to allow the general public to see what Crewe could do. The police had to be called in at 10pm one night to disperse the still waiting crowd. (CT)
142) The unpopularity was largely aimed at the unfavourable bonus allowances allocated to these 'double' engines. (WBB)
145) The man in the smock and trilby is Bob Wooton, who was the Works fitter riding with No. 6202, the 'Turbomotive', for some years in the late 1930s. (CT)
146) The cabs were used for carrying money through the Works but this one looks suspiciously empty. The money was in tins contained in large wooden boxes, which were carried in the cab, stacked where the man in the trilby is standing. (CT)
147) This was probably taken in BR days, judging by the road sign, but it is a moot point. (DB) The Goddard Street buzzer was controlled from the gatehouse behind the large window at the right. (CT)
148) The tyre marks on the concrete road on the right are made by the 'scooters' which replaced the narrow-gauge system. (CT)
160) 28lb sledge hammers helped things straight after the heating as well! (WBB)
162) Six crane runs altogether, one in each bay. (WBB)
165) Stupid boy!!! (WBB) The rumour is that when 71000 went into the Works for tyre-turning after exhibition at the Heritage Centre in 1987, all the big hooks had been scrapped and she could not be lifted. Is this so? (CT)
166) Not necessarily. If you had got both 50 tonners working for you at one time you really cashed in to get things done advantageously. (WBB)
167) It looks as if the rods have just been fitted because the return crank arm is not on and a fitter is securing the leading coupling rod brasses, which were split on this class. The lift of the engine, however, is unique and looks like a special pose for the photographer. (CT)
168) The diesel shunters were worked on in the area west of the traverser (away from the proper steam engines)!, where the saddlers were (who made the leather straps for the windows of the diesel cabs!). (WBB)
173) The machine by the side of the engine is a portable flexible drive grinder for dressing the horns. Before these machines were introduced, the horns were filed square by men sitting on cheese blocks wearing the seats out of their overalls by the constant body movement! (CT)
177) The 'capstan' is a dummy. There were two 100 ton electric winders, one for each half of the shop, for pulling engines out; the wire rope was taken round these dummies for alignment with the shop door. In the belt system introduced in 1926, all engines remained on their own wheels or on slave wheels, and were connected so that the winders had to pull half the belt. (CT)
183) By the clean state of the engine it has probably just left No. 10 shop and has been weighed (the weigh house is out of the picture to the left) before going back to the paint shop, as there are patches of stopping on the cab, firebox, cylinder clothing and running angle. The engine numbers on the smoke deflector and piano plate would be put there before they went outside during repair. Engine numbers on clothing, wheels and so forth, were put on with stencils and had the characteristic stencil break in the figures. The chalk centre marks for valve-setting can be seen on the driving wheels. (CT)
199) The travelling hand crane had turn-down platforms to accommodate two men each side. Usually, they would lift around three tons and some had solid wooden jibs. When I was nineteen, I had one to strip and rebuild. (CT)
203) During the war Horwich was making tanks and Crewe took over maintenance of both the LYR 0-6-0s and the 'Austin 7s'. Several Horwich men and apprentices came to Crewe as well. Crewe made the turrets for Horwich, as well as the complete 'Covenanter' tanks. (CT)
204) The first post-war train to come on the Works was a special for the Institution of Mechanical Engineers in 1947. (CT)
205) The guide is W. H. Taylor, known as 'Bill', who was one of the Works messengers. They were invariably men who had been injured in some way. In Bill's case he had lost an eye following an accident in one of the foundries. In late LNWR days he used to accompany the CME in the Crewe coupe as a servant, making tea and so on. (DB) The other guide was named George but I cannot remember his surname. (CT)
209) The shell of the 'Melts', which was still standing, was used for cutting up. (CT)
210-1) In 210 my father, Ellis Brown, is sitting next but one to the Mayor's left; in 211 he is standing on the footplate holding his trilby, immediately behind the Mayor. When the photos were taken he was Production Manager, Workshops, based at Derby. (DB)
I was there. Three posed groups were photographed on this occasion. A copy of the one with me in it is in our downstairs loo! The then Works Manager, Johnny Barker-Wyatt, is sitting on the Mayor's left. (WBB)

Acknowledgements

In compiling this book, I have enjoyed the help and support of many friends and fellow enthusiasts. David Patrick and Clive Taylor generously offered photographs from their own extensive collections, provided much information, and gave considerable encouragement. Graham Roberts, a former apprentice at the Works, took great trouble to supply information, as also did Harold Froggatt, who drew on his own records and recollections of the late 1930s to assemble details of the shunting engines used in the Works. John Pritchett was extremely helpful and willingly allowed photographs in his collection to be used. John Bucknall, Gordon Davies, David Eatwell and Les Hanson went out of their way to provide photographs which they had taken themselves. W. A. Camwell and W. T. Stubbs kindly arranged for photographs by W. L. Good to be made available, and Peter Ward printed many of them. Tim Shuttleworth also printed many of the pictures. Richard D. Foster, David Ratcliff, Peggy Spibey, Geoff Williams and Ken Wood all helped considerably in various ways.

Credits for the illustrations are as follows (where no credit is given, the photograph is from the author's collection):

BBC Hulton Picture Library: *Plates 48, 59-62, 135, 160-2 and 165.*
British Rail/OPC Joint Venture: *Plates 190-5.*
J. B. Bucknall: *Plates 22, 202 and 205.*
Roger Carpenter Collection: *Plates 78, 164 and 203.*
Gordon Davies: *Plates 19, 210-1.*
David Eatwell: *Plate 213.*
Kenneth Field: *Plate 181.*
W. L. Good: Plates *141-2, 167, 176-7, 182-6, 188-9, 200-1.*
W Hanson: *Plates 2, 136, 143, 168-173, 178, 204, 206-7 and 209.*
LNWR Society Collection: *Frontispiece, Plates 3, 5-18, 21, 25-35, 39, 40, 42, 46-7, 49-58, 63-9, 71, 74, 79, 84-5, 110-22, 125-130, 137-40, 148-51, 153-6, 159, 166, 174-7, 179-81 and 208.*
National Railway Museum, Crown Copyright, reproduced by courtesy of the Keeper: *Figure 1, Plates 38, 41, 80, 124 and 198.*
David Patrick Collection: *Plates 4, 23-24, 43, 51, 131, 144, 147 and 152.*
John Pritchett Collection: *Plates 83-109.*
R. P. Richards, reproduced courtesy of J. P Richards: Plates 44, 81-2 and 133.
Clive Taylor Collection: *Figure 2, Plates 132 and 187.*
As usual, of course, the LNWR Society (membership enquiries to: 3 Chieveley Court, Emerson Valley, Milton Keynes MK4 2DD) played a valuable role in providing moral support and facilitating contact with like minded enthusiasts. To all who have helped in any way I extend my grateful thanks.

Edward Talbot
Stafford, 1986